THE JIM'LL FIX IT STORY

ROGER ORDISH

Hodder & Stoughton
LONDON SYDNEY AUCKLAND

British Library Cataloguing in Publication Data
Ordish, Roger
 The "Jim'll Fix It" story
 I. Title
 791.45

 ISBN 0-340-56619-1

Copyright © Roger Ordish 1992.

First published in Great Britain 1992

All rights reserved. No part of this publication may be reproduced or transmitted in any form or by any means, electronic or mechanical, including photocopying, recording, or any information storage and retrieval system, without either prior permission in writing from the publisher or a licence permitting restricted copying. In the United Kingdom such licences are issued by the Copyright Licensing Agency, 90 Tottenham Court Road, London W1P 9HE. The right of Roger Ordish to be identified as the author of this work has been asserted by him in accordance with the Copyright, Designs and Patents Act 1988.

Published by Hodder and Stoughton,
a division of Hodder and Stoughton Ltd,
Mill Road, Dunton Green, Sevenoaks, Kent TN13 2YA
Editorial Office: 47 Bedford Square, London WC1B 3DP

Photoset by SX Composing, Rayleigh, Essex.

Printed in Great Britain by BPCC Hazells Ltd
Member of BPCC Ltd

CONTENTS

FOREWORD: — 7
Making Dreams Come True
by Sir Jimmy Savile

A PERMANENT FIXTURE — 8

Ten Superlative Fix-Its — 16

FILMING — 18

Ten of the Daftest Things Jim has Fixed — 27

THE STUDIO DAY — 28

THE TEAM — 36

Fourteen Thousand Fixees at Once — 40

WHAT, WHERE AND WHEN? — 42

Sample Survey — 91

DO YOU WANT A GO? — 92

TO SUSIE

Dear World,

Making dreams come true is a really great job. The magic is taking an ordinary request + putting in that extra ingredient that makes it spectacular + memorable. Thats where "Dr Magic" comes into his own.

I used to call him Roger, but Dr Magic is the only true name for the man that makes the Jim'll Fix It dream come true.

This is his story + I bought the first book off the press.

Jimmy Savile

(The man that takes it easy in the chair)

A PERMANENT FIXTURE

Proposals of marriage are not usually televised and Daphne Folan had not expected hers to be, but it was eventually screened to fifteen million viewers. She had agreed to take part in a local television interview on the subject of the sale of council houses, or that was what she thought. Her boyfriend, Mickey, sat on the sofa with her, while the man from the BBC first asked a series of questions on the council house issue. Then her interviewer seemed to change course and his questions took on a more personal nature.

"Excuse me, but are the two of you married?"

"No," replied Daphne.

"Are you likely to get married in the near future?"

"Er, no," said Daphne.

"But what if," the interviewer went on, "what if Mickey got down on one knee and proposed to you this instant. Would you agree to marry him then?"

Daphne could not believe what was going on. "What is this?" she started to protest.

But, as she did so, her boyfriend got off the sofa, knelt down beside her and said, "You have always said that you would agree to marry me only if the wedding took place in the Seychelles. Well, I've got the tickets in my pocket, so you have to say 'yes', when I ask you: Daphne, will you marry me please?"

Daphne looked at Mickey, looked at the interviewer and looked at the camera. She still did not know what was going on, but she gave Mickey a big hug and shouted "Yes!"

A very green wedding: a hand-built chapel, a man-powered organ and no central heating required.

Jim had fixed it for her. Daphne's daughter, Natalie, had written to the programme, explaining how fond the family was of their mum's boyfriend and how happy they would all be if Daphne would accept one of Mickey's endless proposals of marriage. Her mother had put off the decision – indefinitely, she thought, by saying that she would only ever say "yes" if the wedding took place in the romantic Seychelles Islands, three thousand miles away in the Indian Ocean. The whole business about the interview on council house sales had been a set-up, designed by the *Jim'll Fix It* team to capture the great moment on film. A few weeks later, on an island just half a mile across and almost on the Equator, the most idyllic wedding took place. A tropical sun shone on silver sand and azure water. Palm trees swayed in a gentle breeze. A special "chapel" had been built by the locals out of bamboo and palm leaves and a magistrate had flown in just for the occasion to solemnise Daphne's and Mickey's wedding on tiny Bird Island, refuge for several thousand Sooty Terns and a handful of peace-loving human beings.

That was just one of the fifteen hundred or so dreams which Jimmy Savile's "Fix-It" team has made come true over the last seventeen years. Not all of the fixes are as spectacular as Daphne's island wedding. A more typical item in a programme is likely to be a chance to sing along with a favourite pop band or to find out how something is made. But, whatever the request to Jim, it is likely to be of great importance to the person who wrote it and it is one of the jobs of the

The BBC loves initials. We referred to Daphne and Mickey as the HC, the Happy Couple.

Wayne Sleep is Coralie's prince. ("At last I have a partner shorter than me," said the diminutive Wayne.)

Nicola Lowney from Halifax turned into Wonderwoman and tidied her bedroom in thirty seconds thanks to speeded-up film.

production team to try to find an extra twist of excitement for the "Fixee" and – most important of all – entertainment for the licence-fee-paying audience at home.

The programme was the brainchild of Bill Cotton, Junior, son of the famous band-leader, later to achieve fame in his own right as the managing director of BBC Television. In 1975 he was head of the light entertainment section of BBC Television with overall responsibility for anything from *Some Mothers do 'ave 'em* to *Top of the Pops*. He was also constantly on the lookout for new ideas to help in the quest for audiences and quality.

There was a trend towards more public participation in television programmes. Whereas, a few years before, the rather prim *Ask the Family* had been the BBC's only entertainment show with viewer involvement, by 1975 Bruce Forsyth's *Gen-*

eration Game was in its third highly successful series and Esther Rantzen had recently started making public the talents of viewers' singing dogs and comedy carrots in *That's Life*. The time was certainly ripe for a "my wildest dream" slot.

Bill Cotton's decision to ask Jimmy Savile to front the series must also have been influenced by the fact that Jim had already presented two short summer series called *Clunk-Click*. This strange title coincided with a series of TV commercials which were going out at that time, in which Jim exhorted drivers to fasten their seat-belts. "Clunk" was shutting the car door, "Click" was fastening the seat-belt. The series of that name spent part of its time following Jim around Britain, visiting unusual people and places. In the studio-based half of the programme some of the amazing eccentrics, whom Jim had collected on his travels, came to visit and chat to him. Because of the nature of Jimmy Savile some of the items in the *Clunk-Click* programmes turned into "Fix-Its". For example talented young musicians from the Yehudi Menuhin School at Stoke D'Abernon were given the opportunity to perform on television. I remember one particularly brilliant eleven-year-old violinist who appeared. His name was Nigel Kennedy.

Late spring or early summer are the usual times for trying out new programme ideas. If the programme does not work and the weather has been half decent, the show can vanish without trace and most people will be unaware that it was ever on the screen. It was decided to run ten experimental *Jim'll Fix It* shows weekly from April to early June of 1975. Seventeen series later, I think it can be said that the experiment paid off.

Since the show had not been on the air yet, there were of course no requests. So Jimmy was asked to make an appeal for

Singing in the studio with Dannii Minogue. There is so much professionalism, it is hard to spot the Fixee.

letters on *Nationwide*, the popular six o'clock news magazine of the 1970s. He told interviewer Sue Lawley what the programme was to be about and for the first time this address appeared on the screen:

JIM'LL FIX IT
BBC TV CENTRE
WOOD LANE
LONDON W12

A small piece of television history had begun. The response to Jim's first appeal for letters was tremendous, or so it was thought at the time. The BBC postmen dumped sack after sack of mail into the tiny production office until – after a few days – all the chairs had to be put in the corridor. Anyone who came to visit the office was asked to pull up a mailbag and sit down. Then the letter-reading began. The producer and the three researchers sat on their new-found cushions, pulled out the stuffing and read it – letter by letter.

When I now look through a sack of *Jim'll Fix It* mail, I more or less know what to expect. In 1975 the team had no idea of what they were going to find. They would sit there reading in a silence

Jim fixed it for me . . . under water.

Arsenal took on the "Heartline" football team, all of whom have had heart surgery. (The Heartliners won. Can you believe it? Of course you can.)

Weymouth Town Council did the spadework. Sand-artist Fred Darrington did the artwork. The result? A 2,000-ton sandcastle.

of concentration, which would occasionally be broken by such cries as, "Hey, here's someone who wants to swim with a dolphin," or, "There's a boy here who wants to drive a steam engine," – requests which, we now know, can be found at least once in every sack.

There is nothing wrong with those simple ideas, but nowadays they have been asked for so many times that the researchers are usually looking for something a bit more elaborate or original.

A couple of months before the first programme was due to be recorded, the five members of the production team, now joined by a director, had selected what seemed like the most likely two hundred or so letters from the original fifty thousand. Then a BBC conference room was booked for a day and the team sifted through the two hundred, trying to select those requests which would be most likely to catch the audience's interest for the all-important first transmission. A lot of the letters named specific places and activities, which it would not be possible to cover in a television studio. Unless those items were too costly, they could be filmed in advance, but wherever possible Fix-Its would be recorded in the television studio. In the first place it is cheaper, but the studio also has the advantage of a live audience, whose presence should encourage the participants and whose laughter and applause, it is hoped, can add to the enjoyment of the viewers at home. Eventually the contents of the first programme were decided upon.

In 1975 the pinnacle of the pops was surely that remarkable American all-singing family, the Osmonds. As luck would have it, at the time the first *Fix It* was due to be recorded, BBC TV had managed to secure the services of these Mormon wonders for a series of their own. The programmes were being recorded in quick succession over a period of two weeks at the BBC's Television Theatre at Shepherd's Bush Green, London. The Osmonds had one day off in the fortnight

Addressing the problem: part of Jim's 350,000 letter mailbag.

and on that day the Television Theatre was earmarked for the recording of an unheard-of new programme, *Jim'll Fix It*.

Osmond fans were not fully aware of these details and on the day in question there was still a small force of female devotees hovering around Shepherd's Bush Green and looking for any tell-tale signs of an approaching Osmond. A glimpse of white flared trouser emerging from a limo or a distant glint of the setting sun on a Daz-white incisor was enough to set off what was known as the Shepherd's Bush telegraph. Fans would appear, seemingly from nowhere, rushing to wherever they felt they might have the best chance of re-breathing the exhalations of their heroes.

A triumph for *Jim'll Fix It* was that they managed to get the Osmonds to make an appearance on the first programme – not in front of the studio audience for the evening's recording, but the next best thing: a pre-recording in the morning. At about eleven o'clock on the morning of the studio day Osmond followers were only on black alert. They had sensed that an alien programme was in the theatre that day and only the hardiest of followers were on patrol. But they did have some diversion. Jimmy Savile suddenly emerged from the stage door, where they regularly kept their watch. He may not have been an Osmond, but at least he was famous. Little did they know that this was to be only the beginning of an unbelievable day. Jim spoke to three of the girls clustered nearest to the door.

"It's a bit damp out here," he said. "Why not come inside and watch a bit of our rehearsal?"

Naturally the youngsters could not wait to accept Jim's invitation. After all, they would be walking on the very same floor where the Osmonds had trod only yesterday. Jim asked them to sit next to him on set and engaged them in conversation, making sure that they were looking at him and that they would not be aware of anything that went on behind them.

Meanwhile, in a Chinese restaurant adjacent to the TV Theatre, the front and back doors were opened to allow the passage of five hooded figures, who then entered the theatre's scenery dock, cast off their cloaks and waited backstage. Unaware, the girls sat on the stage and chatted nervously to Jim. Their flared jeans and badge-encrusted pastel T-shirts had got damp in the drizzle outside and they were looking a bit bedraggled.

At just the right moment Jim asked them; "And who is it you were hoping to see?"

The reply was a concerted giggle. "The Osmonds."

"Well, why don't you look behind you?" said Jim.

Upstairs in his control room the director shouted, "Cue lights, cue the music, cue the Osmonds!"

Perhaps he should have added, "Stand by the St John Ambulance Brigade," for the girls nearly fainted. The Osmonds sang for them, chatted to them and as a parting gesture gave them the coloured handkerchiefs from the top pockets of their gleaming white suits. If you want to imagine the impact, substitute the name of your musical hero from when you were fifteen.

That was probably the highlight of the first show, but that evening the studio audience seemed to enjoy the rest of the programme. On film they saw Stuart from Andover drive a train, the classic boy's dream of "what I want to be when I grow up". It is impossible to calculate how many times that request has been made since then. Less predictable was Donna Harding's dream. She said she wanted to dig the Channel Tunnel, still an improbability in 1975. Her wish was of course not fulfilled, but she was filmed

After Gemma White's Fix-It which was to find out what happened to the used drinks cans which her form collected, the Alcan corporation offered to make all our badges out of re-cycled aluminium.

A PERMANENT FIXTURE

Mhairi Read from St Albans was the first ever Fixee. Since then tens of thousands have asked for the same thing – swimming with dolphins.

having a try on Ramsgate beach with the aid of some heavy earth-moving equipment. In the studio young Vanessa Cullom danced with Pan's People, then the heart-throbs of every red-blooded male viewer of *Top of the Pops* and a young lady, Gussie van Geest, learned clown make-up. There was an adult in the first ever *Jim'll Fix It* and there have been hundreds since, but some people still express surprise when they see a grown-up on the programme. It is not meant to be a children's programme; it is just that children tend to make good subjects.

There was one more item, the very first to be transmitted in a *Jim'll Fix It*. Mhairi Read from St Albans swam with a dolphin in Windsor Safari Park and ever since then thousands upon thousands have asked to do the same thing. Bill Cotton says of that first transmission: "I remember the first show and the first thing was that girl riding on a porpoise and as I watched it, I thought, We have a hit show here."

He was right.

15

Esmeralda the tortoise, claimed to be the world's oldest living animal.

Ten Superlative Fix Its

1. SURPRISE SUPERSONIC FLIGHT IN A CONCORDE.
   World's fastest airliner.
2. FLOAT IN THE DEAD SEA.
   Place furthest below sea level.
3. MEET MUHAMMAD ALI.
   Boxing's highest ever earner.
4. VISIT BOEING "JUMBO" FACTORY.
   World's largest building.
5. RIDING ON GIANT TORTOISE.
   Claimed as oldest living creature.
6. HAVE CLIFF RICHARD SING TO ME.
   Cliff has had Number One hits in five different decades from the 1950s to the 1990s, a record.
7. VISIT ANGEL FALLS.
   World's highest waterfall.
8. MARCH THROUGH A LOCKHEED C5A GALAXY.
   Largest aircraft in the world.
9. DRIVE THE TGV (TRAIN À GRANDE VITESSE).
   World's fastest passenger train.
10. INTERVIEW MARGARET THATCHER.
    Longest consecutively serving Prime Minister this century.

Fastest plane and fastest train. A Concorde and the high-speed French TGV, le Train à Grande Vitesse.

FILMING

The Fix-Its which need the most planning are those involving a surprise. Take the case of seventeen-year-old Lisa Buckle from North Humberside. Her family are pig-farmers and this is what her mother, Chris, wrote to Jim:

Dear Jim,

Please could you fix it for my daughter Lisa to be Cinderella for a day. She works with the pigs on the farm and spends every day mucking out, cleaning, disinfecting etc. Her working outfit is smelly overalls, big socks, big wellies and a big hat.

Underneath all this is a very pretty, cheerful girl who is happy all day long.

I would love to see her sparkle for a day.

Yours sincerely,
Chris Buckle

Our policy on surprises in *Jim'll Fix It* is that we try not to make a fool of anybody. This seemed an ideal opportunity for a surprise which would be both pleasant and a lot of fun for the family concerned. One of the first things I had to do on my secret preliminary visit to the farm was to ask Mrs Buckle how her daughter would respond to the sudden appearance of a fully fledged Fairy Godmother in her pigsty.

"Oh, she'll forgive me," I was told.

I could tell they were a loving family and that there was no element of trickery in their intentions. We decided to go for a surprise. But, how to do it?

In the old days of *Candid Camera* the camera often had to be hidden, and concealing a camera creates problems. First there is the difficulty of finding a hiding-place and, once the camera is in its hide, it cannot be moved. There is a fair chance that your victims will end up standing with their backs to the camera. But now in the age of the home video people are far more used to seeing movie-cameras around them as everyday objects and all that is needed is a little white lie as to who you are and why you are there.

In the case of the Buckle family they had recently been visited by a camera crew from the Shell Oil Company, who were making a promotional film about their agricultural products. I decided that we would pretend to be the Shell Film Unit, making a return visit to the farm to take some extra shots. (I hope their director will forgive me for implying that they failed to get all the shots they needed during their first visit.)

Although the pigsties were "free-range", they were inside a big barn. We would be needing plenty of electric light – make a note of that. Cinderella has to go to a ball. Did her mum have any suggestions about that? As luck would have it every Saturday night a lot of young people in that area gather at the Patrington Caravan Club for a mixture of live music and disco. I could picture it at once: our Fairy Godmother must say, "You *shall* go to the Caravan Club dance." (With a bit of luck Lisa would reply, "But I was going there anyway.")

I did not meet Lisa on this first secret visit, but Mrs Buckle was able to show me a home video of her daughter. Lisa certainly was a good-looking young lady

Lisa: (thinks) "Oh how I wish..."

Fairy Godmother: "You shall go to the ball!" Lisa: "And what do the pigs get turned into? Coachmen?" Fairy Godmother: "No, the wedding breakfast."

Pig: "Oh, very funny."

and would provide a great opportunity for our make-up and costume designers to glam her up for the evening of the great day.

So at the conclusion of our first meeting Lisa's mother and I had decided a "yes" and a "where" and a "when". Over the next few weeks I made a few more secret calls to Chris, announcing myself always as the man from the Shell Film Unit. I decided to modernise and simplify the plot: there would be a pumpkin and just one mouse. Rather than turning into a carriage and coachman, they would become a car and chauffeur. I needed to know what was Lisa's favourite car. (A Lotus.) Make a note of that. Call the Lotus car company. Could they provide a car? (They could. And a chauffeur.) What were Lisa's measurements, what were her favourite colours, what type of man should we look for in her Prince Charming? ("Hunky," said her mother confidently.)

A suitably hunky Prince Charming was cast (actor Mark Heenehan) and for our Fairy Godmother we managed to secure the services of Rachel Bell (familiar to viewers of *Dear John* and *The Darling Buds of May*). A film crew and lighting crew had to be hired, accommodation found locally for everyone and I had to write a script. The script for something like this cannot be written to the exact word. For instance who knows what the title role, Cinderella, is going to say?

In this case, Cinderella did not say very much as things turned out. There she was in the sty, minding the pigs' business, so to speak, when out from behind a forklift truck sprang Rachel in full fairy queen regalia plus wand and wellies.

"You shall go to the ball," she cried.

Lisa was dumbfounded, but, as her mother had predicted, she cheerfully entered into the spirit of the occasion – even when we caught her a second time.

Under the throbbing disco lights of the Caravan Club Lisa had the camera trained on her as she chatted to a girlfriend. Stealthily from behind Lisa approached Mark the Magnificent as Prince Charming in a splendid early nineteenth-century-style military outfit. He looked like Beau Brummel's younger, smarter brother.

He bent down, took Lisa's hand in his and announced, "I'm Charming, Prince Charming," to which Lisa replied, "I'm flabbergasted," which was a much better "punchline" than anything I could have written.

Fairy Godmother: "Don't stand too near the pumpkin or you might get a back tyre on your toes."

FILMING

Cinderella finds her Prince quite charming.

Grant teaches Kerry the tricks of the tourist trade and demonstrates the latest local dance craze, "La Sopa de Caracol".

The requests people send to *Jim'll Fix It* concern themselves generally with whims and wild dreams, not with long-term ambitions, but there are exceptions. I hope, for instance, that nine-year-old Keiran Leigh will one day really be a researcher on the consumer magazine, *Which?*, as he was briefly two years ago. I should also like to think that Daniel Nicholson will become a wildlife photographer which was what he did for two wonderful days in Africa in 1989. But one career Fix-It I am certain of, if she can make the grade, is the case of sixteen-year-old Kerry Woodward from near Coventry. She wrote to Jim asking to be a holiday courier, having seen couriers at work while she was on a camping holiday in France.

Kerry's Fix-It trip took her a bit further away from home than that – to the tropical rain-forest of South America, where she helped to lead a small band of adventurous British holidaymakers up a tributary of the giant Orinoco River in Venezuela.

These tourists were on a day trip from resorts on the island of Margarita, which is part of Venezuela and is situated just off its coast in the extreme south of the Caribbean Sea. That is also where Kerry was based for her all-too-brief courier job-experience. The whole trip was completed in just under a week. It is exciting to go to these distant glamorous locations, but I believe the following timetable will show that it can be pretty busy as well:

Tuesday Twelve-hour flight London-Paris-Margarita.

Wednesday Kerry has concentrated courier lessons from local Falcon resort director, Grant Holmes, a young Englishman with several years of courier experience behind him. Kerry: "Grant is so enthusiastic about his work. His confidence is infectious and he makes me able to do things I thought I wasn't capable of."

FILING

Thursday

Meanwhile BBC director finds locations for filming on the island, researcher arranges flights for Kerry and film crew to mainland for Saturday.
Evening: Venezuelan film crew arrives by air from capital city, Caracas.

Friday

9.00 a.m.: Filming Kerry as she continues to have lessons from Grant. To start with she is giving a tour-talk to an empty village square. Next she has to try it with real holidaymakers.
Noon: Filming exterior shots of the tour on its way to the nearest location.
1.30 p.m.: Filming Kerry helping to supervise serving of a seafood lunch in a beach restaurant.
3.30 p.m.: Filming Kerry telling bus passengers she is taking them to a seafood lunch in a beach restaurant. (As with all filming, things are done in the wrong order.)

Kerry: "Welcome aboard, ladies and gentlemen . . . this is your driver, José. Say 'hello', José . . . José has especially asked you not to smoke while you are on the tour bus. We are on our way to one of the best-known beaches in Venezuela, Playa el Agua." (Thinks: Phew, I got my tongue round that one, but soon I have to start telling them about the Guacaree Indians.)

Saturday

3.45 a.m. (note a courier's working hours): All rise early to get to the airport for a 6.00 a.m. take-off. The twenty-seater, twin-engined Dornier is away on time for a two-and-a-half-hour flight to the "Indian" village of Kavac. Kerry is not just a passenger. She is at work, microphone in hand, just as if she was in a bus.

"Sorry about the noise, ladies and gentlemen, I hope you can hear me at the back . . . shortly, if you look out of the left-hand side of the aircraft, you will see Angel Falls, the world's highest waterfall. Those on the right don't worry. In a minute we shall fly back in the other direction, so you will be able to take pictures too . . . Our destination is Kavac . . . There are no roads into Kavac. We have to fly into the grass landing-strip, where you will have the opportunity to marvel at the table-top mountains, reminiscent of the 'Lost World' of Sir Arthur Conan Doyle." The reason that

Condor's eye view of the Angel Falls (the world's highest waterfall).

The film crew try to keep their camera dry.

Saturday *cont.*

Kerry was able to manage all of the above without stumbling once could be that Grant Holmes was one of her passengers, doing a sort of constant tic-tac for her, to remind Kerry what to say next.

9.00 a.m.: The next part of the trip is so specialised that the couriers, although still on duty, hand over to the Indian guides. The guides, wearing only their loincloths, lead the customers on foot along the trail into the rain-forest. The tourists are not wearing much more than their guides – trainers, swimming costumes and sun-tan lotion. The sun-tan lotion is washed off again at the first stop on their journey, where everyone takes a natural cold shower halfway up a hundred-foot waterfall. And there is a lot more water ahead.

10.30 a.m.: Kerry is in action again, trying to remember the lines Grant has been teaching her, as she stands in front of her group, gathered on top of a flat rock beside the rushing river.

"Release the stress of city life. Jump off this rock into the torrent below. It's only five metres down!" A courier cannot tell her group to jump off a rock unless she jumps too. So off she goes.

12.30 p.m.: The intrepid travellers follow the river (and Kerry) upstream into the Sacred Cave, a cave which has a massive waterfall inside it. The chasm is so narrow and the current therefore so strong that only the most powerful swimmers can make it to the waterfall. Kerry manages to get there with the aid of ropes attached to bolts, which have been drilled into the rocks on one side. It is worth the effort for the more adventurous, who get to the enclosed falls. Kerry could not speak to the group now if she wanted to. The thunder of the water drowns even their shrieks of delight as the cascading droplets massage their sun-tanned backs.

2.30 p.m.: Make sure all present and content at a late barbecue lunch inside the large straw-roofed dining hut. What kind of steaks are these? Iguana? Brontosaurus from the Lost World? (Best South American beef, actually.)

3.30 p.m.: Take off for Margarita again with an essential refuelling stop at Ciudad Bolivar en route.

7.00 p.m.: Return exhausted party to their hotels. "Where can we go tomorrow? What tours are available? I can't open the fridge in our bedroom; can you help?"

Phew! Who'd be a courier? Kerry would. Good luck to her, and I mean it.

FILMING

The "Indian" guides lend a hand and give advice.

Kerry qualifies and earns her courier's uniform.

Four giant Welsh pigeons formate for the Birdie Dance. Nelson turned a blind eye.

FILMING

Ten of the daftest things Jim has fixed

1. Jump a horse trials course (without a horse).
2. Go to work in bed.
3. Shear a sheep to look like a poodle.
4. Be a pantomime horse in a horse-race.
5. Order a marmalade and sausage sandwich at the Savoy Hotel.
6. Be a yoghurt in a fridge.
7. Do the Birdie Dance in Trafalgar Square, dressed as pigeons.
8. Make funny faces through the studio windows at Pebble Mill.
9. Wash Rod Hull's Emu's neck.
10. Have a song sung to our goat.

Adrian Grain, the incredible eventing man. (Adrian, a farmer, owns a successful race-horse, Shepherd's Hymn. Why keep a horse and jump yourself?)

THE STUDIO DAY

Jimmy Savile joins Anita Brealey and "The Fairer Sax" during a break in rehearsal.

The day we record our programmes in the studio really begins the previous night. The working space at the BBC Television Centre is in use most of the time and more often than not the day before a *Jim'll Fix It* recording, the studio will have been used for another programme. It may have been a drama, a quiz programme or a situation comedy. All the scenery and furniture of that show must be taken out of the studio and our set must be moved in. The "striking" or removal of the old set is done by the night scene crew, the bane of the set designers. These crews sometimes have the reputation of working through as little of the night as possible by getting the old scenery out extremely quickly and therefore not very carefully. If the set is for a series it is the designer's job to make the scenery look brand-new again for the same day the following week.

With luck most of the set is up by the time the members of the camera crew arrive at 9.30 a.m. The lighting crew are already at work, setting the lamps as plotted by the lighting director, and the engineers are checking that the heavily used electronic apparatus is still in perfect working order. At 10.30 it is time for rehearsal to start. Helen Gartell, the director, sits at the control-room desk and checks that the floor manager, Quentin, can hear her on the talkback system.

"Can we have cameras on cans, please?" she says (i.e. will the camera crew members please put their headsets on). Sitting next to the director is the vision mixer, who is studying the camera script. She controls the apparatus which cuts or mixes from one camera's output to another. Some of these cuts have already been marked in the script by the director, but in an ad-lib situation such as the chat between Jimmy and his guests there is just a list of shots as opposed to a sequence. Here is an example:

Camera 1   Mid-shot   Carl Hester, or 2-s Helen/Carl
Camera 2   Mid-shot   Helen Gronow
Camera 3   Three-shot
Camera 4   Mid-shot   Jimmy Savile

The actual cutting sequence depends on how the conversation moves and is usually at the discretion of the vision mixer. The director is keeping an eye out for what is going to happen next. She may say, for example, "Stand by to widen on camera one. Jim's about to go for the badge."

"The Fairer Sax" keep viewers "In the Mood".

Children, brothers and sisters of the briefly famous sit in the "specially invited" section of the studio audience.

But all that will happen much later in the day. At the moment we are at the plodding stage of the rehearsal. To the casual observer nothing seems to be happening. In fact there is a lot going on, but the rehearsal can proceed only at the speed of the contributor who needs the most time. One of the things that makes working in television so interesting is that you very seldom do exactly the same thing twice. Rehearsal is a gradual coming together. Here is a typical example of that process.

The lighting director might say to the director, "If you take that shot of him, you'll get a boom shadow on his face" (a shadow of the pole which carries the microphone). There are then a number of options as to how to get round the problem:

1. Move the person to another place.
2. Take the shot from another position.
3. Reposition the boom which is causing the shadow while still being able to hear the person.
4. Relight the shot, so that the boom shadow lands elsewhere.

As you can imagine, it all takes time, but there is not a lot of time to play with, so

whenever possible, while A sorts out his problem, B tries to move on to find out what his next problem is going to be.

At 11.00 a.m. the first performers arrive. Anita Brealey, aged seventeen, has been learning to play the saxophone for just two years and – rather courageously – she wrote to Jim asking for the chance to play with that brilliant all-female trio, the Fairer Sax. Anita has already had two rehearsals, one ten days ago, so that she had time to practise at home, and one yesterday to consolidate it all. Today's rehearsal is not so much for the performers as for the machinery and the people who operate it. And it all feels very different for Anita. It is the first time for her in front of lights, cameras and microphones and the first time in costume, not jeans and T-shirt but a satin dress to blend with those of the other players.

A first television studio rehearsal can

How the magic carpet looks to the studio audience . . .

be fairly off-putting for a performer. There you are, giving of your best, while those all around you appear to be taking no notice of you. They are just getting on with their jobs, adjusting a lamp or a microphone, repainting a bit of the floor or even knocking nails noisily into a bit of scenery. The floor manager approaches. At last someone is going to speak to you. As he reaches you, all of a sudden his eyes glaze over. He does speak – but not to you. It is as if he is addressing an apparition, visible only to him.

"Yes, yes, a bit to the right? Yes, okay."

He is in fact conversing with the director. She Who Must Be Obeyed is talking to him via his minute earpiece. Finally he is free to talk to you: "Could you stand a little bit over to your left, dear. Try to make sure you can feel the light from that lamp on your face. Oh, and the director says, 'Try not to scowl!' Right! Quiet everybody! From the top once again."

It's not easy. All too soon Anita's camera rehearsal time is up and the next studio item for today's programme must be set in and rehearsed. Six-year-old Charlotte Howarth's Fix-It is a very different affair. "Please can you fix it," she had written, "to make it look like I am flying?" (Sensible girl – no ideas about really flying, just "Can you make it look like . . .?") I should not say, "No problem!" but rather "Lots of little, surmountable problems".

. . . and how the effect looks to the viewers at home. Charlotte at speed off the Highland Coast.

Jimmy Savile with studio cameraman, John Sherlock. (While still at school, John wanted to be a television cameraman. There was no Jim to write to then. He went about fulfilling his ambition. After "A" levels in physics and maths, he worked as an assistant electrician in the theatre. He kept knocking on the door of the BBC who finally offered him a job: trainee camera assistant. Two years later, he qualified.)

The members of the scene crew bring into the centre of the studio a large wooden block. This they then cover with a green baize cloth, which is also draped over a screen behind the block. If a camera looks head-on at this scene it now sees nothing but greenness. A Persian carpet is laid on top of the block and Charlotte in a lovely "Arabian Nights" outfit sits on the carpet. There is no green in the carpet and no green in Charlotte's costume.

A colour television camera is really three cameras in one containing a tube to "read" each of the primary colours, red, blue and green. Using a system called colour separation overlay all the green part of the picture coming from the camera can be replaced on the transmission screen with information from another source. For this other source I was able to borrow part of a fascinating BBC Television programme, called *The Shape of the Nation*, for which the Royal Air Force had attached cameras to a fighter plane, which then flew all round the nation's coastline to create a sort of living map. So, while Charlotte's carpet is really on a bit of green cloth it appears to be flying round the coast of Britain at twelve hundred miles an hour. It takes a bit of time and much electronic tweaking to make this process look right, but little Charlotte keeps smiling through it all. A final touch is added by hooking some fishing line on to the fringe of the carpet so that it can be made to flap in the "breeze".

THE STUDIO DAY

We have reached one o'clock. It is the lunch break. Today's three other Fixees arrive about this time. These are the people whose Fix-Its have already been filmed. There is ten-year-old Alys Jones, who wanted to be a nun for a day, eighty-two-year-old Fred Baber, who with his granddaughter went back as a pupil to the school he first attended seventy-one years ago and Helen Gronow at whose seventeenth birthday party Jimmy Savile had made a surprise appearance ten years after he had been invited. Before they have their lunch all the Fixees go to a sound recording studio in another part of the building to record the words of the letters they wrote to Jim all that time ago. A problem arises. Although Alys Jones wanted to be a nun when she wrote her letter, she no longer wants to be one, she says. Being – not surprisingly - a young lady with high moral principles, she is unwilling to read out that which is no longer true. Researcher David Matthew manages to persuade her that she will only be re-creating what was true at the time of writing.

While all this is happening Jimmy Savile's taxi arrives at the BBC Television Centre. I meet him in the reception area and we go to his star dressing-room to discuss today's programme. There I show him a running order of the programme, photocopies of the letters and the cards which he will have to hand during the programme and which tell him what should be happening when and where. It is relaxed and informal and more like a chat than a business meeting. There is usually a queue of people waiting to see Jimmy Savile after we have finished: families of hospital connections, radio reporters or journalists eager for an interview. His dressing-room is one of the few places where they can track him down.

I leave Jim to his visitors and go to the sound recording studio to record the voice of Jim's chair. When this robotic masterpiece hands Jim a badge the chair usually makes a comment on the proceedings. For instance today it will tell birthday girl Helen that it has been waiting ten years for this moment and remind magic carpeteer Charlotte that she has left her carpet on a double yellow line.

At about 3.00 p.m., the studio is ready for the run-through with Jim. There are already about twenty people sitting in the audience, mostly family and friends of Fixees. A buzz goes up as Jim enters. There are now two and a half hours to check every detail of what will be happening this evening: shots, lighting, sound, picture quality, machines to play film and videotape into the studio, design, make-up, costume props and giant TV screens to show the studio audience the filmed inserts. Today there are more than forty people working exclusively on the preparation of this programme. If it goes well, it should look as if it required no effort at all. To that end Jimmy Savile helps to put all our guests at their ease. They are our most important commodity. If they enjoy the programme, there is more chance that the viewers at home will. I confer with the production assistant in the control gallery as to how long she thinks the programme will be. The finished product is supposed to be thirty-four and a quarter minutes long. If it seems to be too long, we may have to postpone an item until another week. On the rare occasions when we look like under-running I have to ask Jim to increase the chat (no problem). Tonight it looks as if the show will run to the right duration.

We have to finish rehearsals by 5.30 p.m. to allow for a final technical check on the equipment. Then at six o'clock the doors are opened to admit the studio audience, usually parties of people whose organisers have written to the BBC's

ticket unit asking for some of the free tickets available for various shows. Perhaps because the tickets are free some of the audience do not turn up, especially if it is a cold, wet night. There should be three hundred and fifty people in the audience. If there are not, the job of making it sound as if there were goes to the "warm-up man". For us this is Felix Bowness, well known to fans of *Hi-de-Hi* as Fred Quilley, the jockey. He chats the audience into a relaxed and friendly mood.

Looking at his list which tells him what parties are in tonight's audience, he says, "Right, I want the party from the Hoover factory to stand up and say, 'Good evening' to the Second Sutton Scouts. Come on. 'Good evening, Sutton Scouts.' That's right. Now, Sutton Scouts stand up and say, 'Good evening, Hoover factory'." Much laughter. Then he tells everyone to turn round and shake hands with the person behind them. They all turn, but there is no hand to shake, since the person behind has also turned round.

"Ladies and gentlemen," says Felix, "here he is, Sir Jimmy Savile!"

Jim enters to a cheer. He is no longer in his rehearsal tracksuit. Now it is a smart blazer and chinos. One of the sound crew conceals a radio microphone and transmitter in Jim's clothing and floor manager Quentin announces, "We are running up to record," meaning that the two video recording machines are being brought to a state where they can receive a steady picture.

Jim sits in his famous chair, and on a signal from Quentin turns to camera one and makes his weekly announcement: "Good evening, ladies and gentlemen and welcome to some more super 'Jim'll Fix-Its'." The opening titles roll.

If all goes well, less than an hour later everything will be in the can, but Jim temporarily fools the studio audience by saying, "Well that was okay for rehearsal; now we do it for real." Then he adds, "Goodnight, safe journey home."

Jimmy Savile gets ready for his 267th recording of Jim'll Fix It.

The audience during the "warm-up". "We'll be turning the cameras on you," says Felix, "so if you're sitting next to someone you shouldn't be, now's the time to change your place."

THE TEAM

Jim's team varies in size according to the time of year. There are periods when only two people are working exclusively on this programme: myself and a researcher. When we are in the middle of the run of recording the studio shows the number goes up to six: producer, director, two researchers, production assistant and AFM (assistant floor manager). The duties of researchers depend very much on the

The Maharajah of Jodhpur lent Shefali Bates his palanquin (and bearers) so that she could become a "Maharanee for a day".

type of programme they are doing. On *Jim'll Fix It* one of the first tasks is telephoning the Fixees and going to interview them. The purpose of these visits is to make sure that the person who wrote is suitable and genuine. We are not looking for beautiful, well-behaved starlets. We want a cross-section of ordinary people, but sometimes there are applicants who unfortunately have to be rejected.

Some of the youngsters have turned out to be unmanageably shy, clinging to mum's apron and unable to speak except through her. It is a difficult judgment to make because many children behave very differently at home from how they perform in front of a camera in a strange environment. Mostly they blossom when their parents are not there and we usually ask parents to make themselves scarce when their offspring are being filmed. Young Ben Strange was quite a chatty lad when our researcher visited him at his home. On camera, playing tennis with Virginia Wade, he uttered not a single word during an hour's filming.

Some people change their minds and when the researcher visits them will say something like, "When I wrote, I didn't think I'd ever get selected." Others are honest enough to admit that since writing they no longer think the pop band or whatever had taken their fancy is the best thing since sliced bread. If the Fix-It requires a bit of a performance, the researcher may visit a number of potential Fixees in order to discover who has the most potential as a singer or dancer.

Once the selection has been made the Fixee becomes the special charge of the researcher, who will organise their travel, accommodation and the details of their Fix-It. The two researchers this year are Gabrielle Jackson and David Matthew. David has got the job he wanted and he worked very hard to get it. A lot more want to work for the BBC than the BBC has room for and what David had to go through in order to work where he does, shows how stiff the competition is. When he left school he was uncertain of what he wanted to do and had settled for a course at art college. One evening during his first term he had managed to get his hands on that rare commodity, a ticket for *Top of the Pops* and went along just to see what it

Bricklaying in the Arctic.

The appropriately named Pamela Hailstone and the author by her finished igloo.

would be like. He did not know what a momentous event it would turn out to be, because in that studio he was to make a decision which would affect the rest of his career. He saw the lights, I suppose you could say. "This is where I want to work," he decided.

He was determined to get his foot in the BBC door one way or another. As luck would have it, a few weeks later an advertisement appeared in the Shepherd's Bush job centre: "BBC holiday relief scenic operative required, seven-day fortnight." David applied for the job and got it. The "seven-day fortnight" meant seven twelve-hour working days out of every fourteen, setting up and striking heavy scenery and props in the studios at the Television Centre. It was hard work, but David enjoyed it and he was where he wanted to be. It gave him the opportunity to look around, see other television people at their various jobs and to decide what line of work he should aim for next. Rather than being a cameraman or a technician, he was most attracted to a job on a production team. He managed to secure an informal interview with one of the studio management staff and was advised, "Stay here and be very lucky or try to

Seasoned researcher, Gabrielle Jackson, contemplates a filming schedule.

enter the production side of the corporation by the 'traditional method'." This would mean two years on a stage management course at a top drama school, followed by at least two years' work in the professional theatre. After that he would be entitled just to apply for the humblest job, floor assistant, and they could give him no guarantee that he would get a job.

It was a tough decision, but David opted for the "traditional method" and was accepted by a London drama college, LAMDA. After a hard two-year course he had to go in search of the second requirement, the professional theatre experience – not the easiest thing to find. However he achieved it and after a year of "earning peanuts on tour" as he puts it, David qualified at last for the precious Equity union card and was thereafter entitled to work on (or behind) the West End stage, eventually landing a job as assistant stage manager on that massive hit, *Les Misérables*. After nearly a year of that he was in a position to apply for a BBC job. After several applications he was finally offered a six-month "holiday relief" contract as a floor assistant. It meant halving his income, but such was his keenness that he took the job. Three years later he was to find himself as the assistant floor manager on none other than *Top of the Pops*, the very programme which had inspired him seven years before. He later did the AFM job on *Jim'll Fix It*, which was where I got to know him and was pleased to be able to offer him a researcher post when a vacancy arose.

Gabrielle Jackson, our other researcher, started on *Jim'll Fix It* in 1980. She left the show in 1985 and went on to do grander and higher-paid jobs for ITV, such as associate producer on *Cluedo* and *Busman's Holiday*. I was delighted to be able to welcome her back when she offered her services once again last year, saying, "It's just that I have never worked on a programme I have enjoyed so much as this one." It is the variety of the work that appeals to her. Tasks she remembers fondly include:

- Having to find a deserted island in the Bahamas so that young brothers Ben and Marcus Green could spend a night alone on it.

- Trying to hide an elephant in a small Somerset village without a bride and groom discovering that it was to be their wedding conveyance the following day.

- Driving a brand-new Rolls-Royce belonging to the manufacturers around London, because their chauffeur kept losing his way when trying to locate Jimmy Savile's flat.

A less fond memory is of being vomited on by an overfed Fixee in a sweet factory. But I guess on the whole the good bits must have outweighed the bad.

Our director, Helen Gartell, is a deter-

mined lady. When she set out as a secretary in BBC Radio, her stated ambition was one day to be a producer. The reaction she got tended to be a polite smile or a verbal pat on the head. After grammar school Helen took a two year business course at the Manchester College of Commerce. The college was situated near the BBC's local television studio, a converted chapel in Dickinson Road. Watching the comings and goings from this studio awoke a keen interest in Helen and she wrote to the BBC in London, asking what job opportunities they might have for her. After she obtained her diploma they were able to give her a post as secretary in their publicity department. Helen was in the BBC but not the right bit of it, programme production. Via an internal job advertisement she eventually became a production secretary in music programmes for Radio Two (the *Ted Heath Band Show* for example). After a couple of years she managed to make the jump to television, becoming a production assistant in the light entertainment department and working on such shows as *Morecambe and Wise*, *The Generation Game* and *The Paul Daniels Magic Show*.

In 1985 she was promoted to production manager, a sort of number two to the producer, but her target of directing or producing still eluded her and after a year or so in that role she bravely resigned and went freelance. It was not an easy time and Helen had to take what work she could find, which included more lowly jobs than she had been doing at the BBC. But she survived and finally got a short contract back with the BBC to produce the viewers' letters programme, *Points of View*. After a year of that she came to join us on *Jim'll Fix It*.

What is the difference between a producer and a director? A producer is responsible for the budget of a programme and has the ultimate say in what its contents are, as does an editor in a newspaper or a magazine. A director literally calls the shots when out filming or in the television studio. In some programmes the director and producer are the same person. On *Jim'll Fix It* there are two separate people for the two jobs. As producer I decide after consultation with the rest of the team which Fix-Its we shall do. Then Helen and I, each working with one of the researchers, direct about half each of the forty-five filmed stories we need for a series. On our studio recording days Helen directs the five or six studio cameras, while I supervise the content of the programme and Jim's part in it, as well as attempting to make the show run to the right duration. In fact we usually aim to make the programme a little too long, so that at the final videotape edit the programme can be tightened and improved for its forthcoming transmission. It is part of my job to decide exactly what bits get cut out and what bits get left in. But I never let any of our Fixees become the face on the cutting-room floor.

On an Anglesey beach for the "summer Christmas" film director Helen Gartell calls the shots while researcher David Matthew consults.

Fourteen thousand Fixees at once

It was the biggest ever. Last summer Jeff Evans wrote to Jim on behalf of all the inhabitants of Holyhead, North Wales. He was asking for an extra Christmas, because most of the Holyheadians had gone down with a particularly nasty flu virus the Christmas before. In his letter Jeff described their festive season as: "Turkey in the bin or dog, kids playing alone with their toys because dad's ill. Xmas carols – stop that noise!"

With a great deal of help from the townspeople the *Fix-It* team created a summer Christmas in the middle of August. There were carol-singers in bathing costumes, barbecued turkey on the beach and tinsel everywhere glittering in the summer sun. Frank Bruno made a striking Father Christmas and was ably assisted by his helper, Ruth Madoc, in bringing some unseasonal festivity to town and the beaches. It was ho-ho-ho hot!

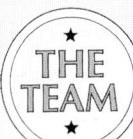

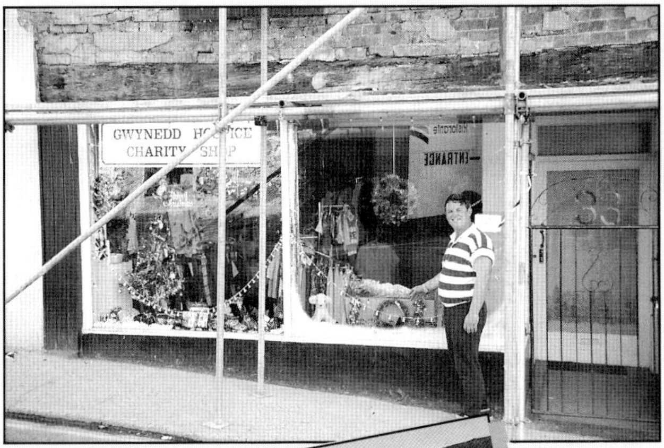
CHARITY SHOP

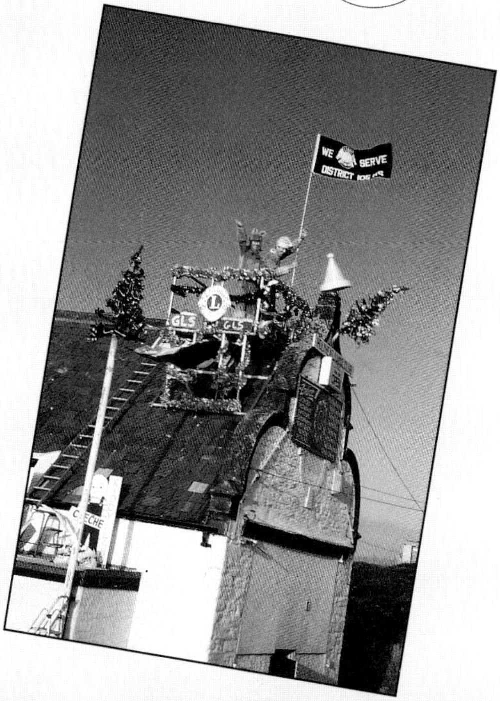
WE SERVE
GLS GLS

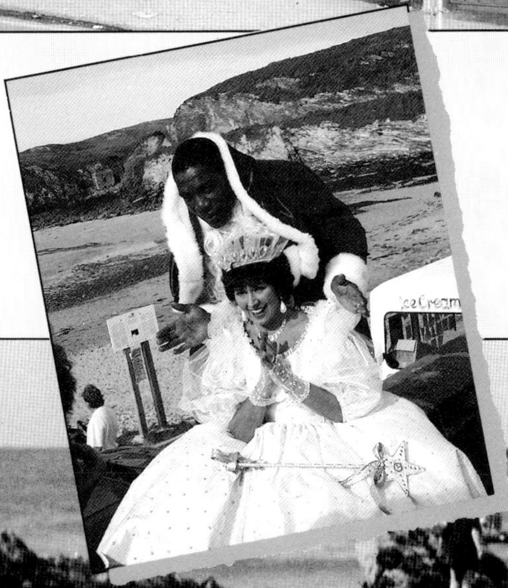

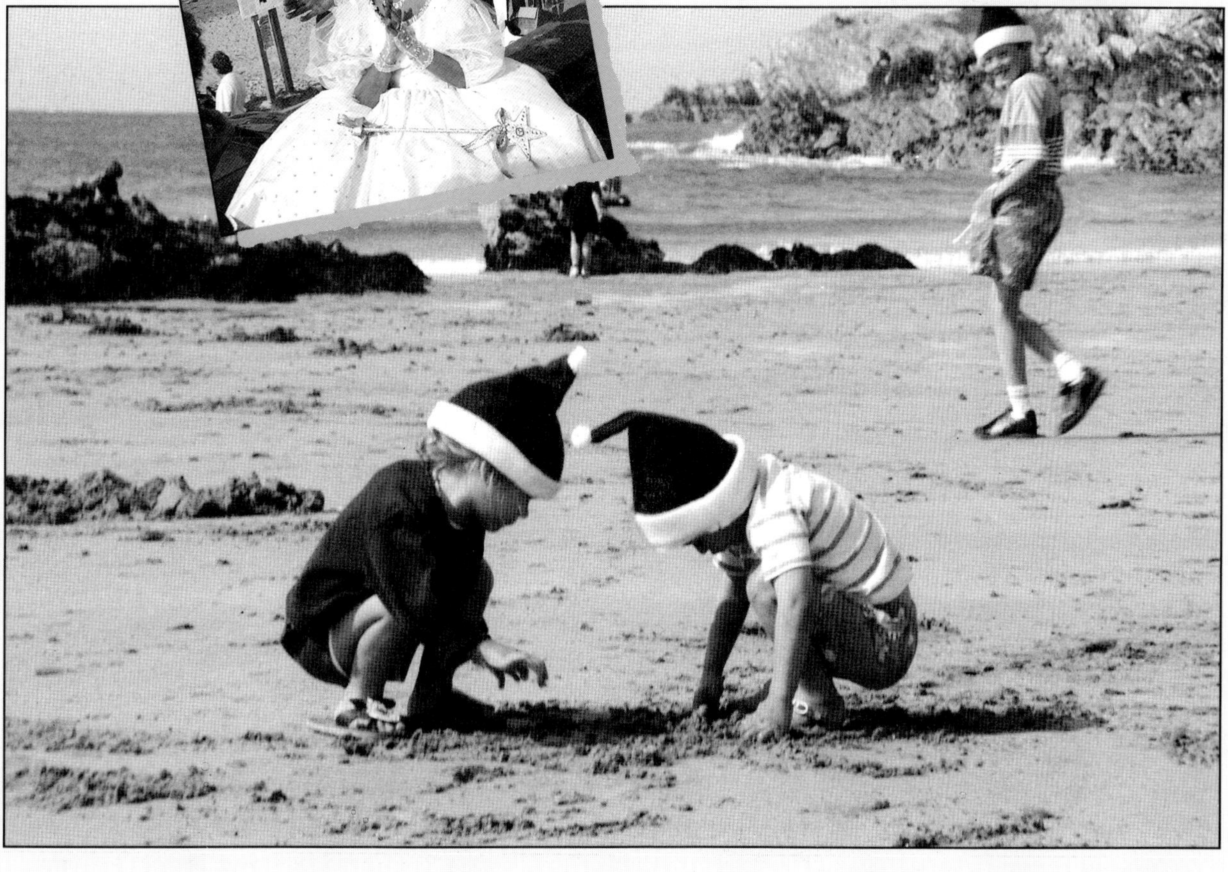

WHAT, WHERE AND WHEN?

On the next few pages I have attempted to answer the questions most frequently asked about *Jim'll Fix It*.

Q: WHAT IS JIMMY SAVILE REALLY LIKE?

I have started with the hardest one to answer, because despite his extrovert public image Jimmy is quite a private person and only a few people know him well. If I take the question to mean, "What is he like to work with?" then – from a producer's point of view – he makes the ideal presenter. He takes a keen interest in everything that goes on and I keep him informed of what we are up to, but he lets his team get on with the day-to-day working of the programme. If I am in any doubt about the suitability of an item, I will immediately consult Jim. Having worked together for eighteen years, we know each other's thinking, or I think we do.

A fairly frequent request is to tread grapes with bare feet. Knowing Jim's strong views on alcohol abuse, I had always ignored this request. Then one day someone thrust a grape-treading letter directly into Jim's hands and he said to me he reckoned it would make a good Fix-It. "She's only going to tread them," he said. "She doesn't have to drink them."

I have worked in the past with presenters who did not trust their production teams and wanted a complete and detailed say on who and what was in their

Indescribable?
Unflappable?
Ineffable?
Unfoolable?

"After all, it's only television," says Jim.

shows. The effect of this approach can be that, if a person drops out of a programme or if an item has to be cancelled, the whole production team grinds to a halt until the presenter has finished playing golf or can be dragged out of a dinner-party. Bill Cotton believes that the main reasons for the long life of the programme are Jimmy Savile's personality and his method of working.

Jimmy Savile's television performance is so relaxed it is easy to imagine that it requires no effort. What would throw him? One of our Fix-Its in 1980 involved a twelve-year-old girl and her mother. The daughter had written to ask if someone could teach her mother to take photographs properly. She had enclosed some examples of her mother's pictures, most of which decapitated the subject. We managed to secure the services of Patrick Lichfield and the Kodak Museum of Photography. For the filming the mother and daughter and Lord Lichfield were dressed in early Victorian costume and Patrick illustrated amongst other things how the subject of a portrait would have to sit with her head in a clamp so as to stay sufficiently still for the lengthy exposures required in those days. It was an interesting and entertaining little film and, when it became part of a programme some months later, it was shown, as are all the films, to the studio audience.

The BBC Television Theatre was packed to its three hundred and fifty capacity. Jimmy Savile introduced the girl's letter of request and then the film. The studio lights were dimmed so that the audience could concentrate on the television screens hung above their seats. The director in the control room gave the instruction "Run telecine!" and the film duly appeared on the screens. The floor assistant brought on to the stage the people involved in the film, to whom Jimmy would be talking after its projection. Despite the dim lighting I could see that Jim was beckoning to me. I tiptoed hastily over to his chair and he whispered to me, "Who's that sitting next to Patrick Lichfield?"

I looked along the line of guests. Next to Jim was the girl, and then the girl's mother, the failed photographer. Next to her sat Lord Lichfield and next to him another man, whom I had never seen in my life.

There were only about two minutes of the film left to run, but I had to reply, "I'm afraid, I don't know, Jim. I shall have to go and ask him."

I envisaged the awkward, whispered conversation that would ensue: "Excuse me. I am the producer of this programme. Can you please tell me who you are?"

"How dare you? I'm Lord Kodak!"

However Jim saved me the embarrassment. "Don't bother. Leave it to me. I'll work it out."

So Jim was prepared to interview someone whom his producer was unable to identify. It turned out to be Patrick's assistant, who had appeared heavily bewhiskered in the film and was now unrecognisably clean-shaven. All went smoothly, but I have since wondered if someone with sufficient nerve could create a bit of fame if not fortune for themselves by slipping on to the end of the sofa just before a chat show went live on to the air. Perhaps one of my readers would like to have a try, but don't say I sent you . . .

Jim is a busy man and *Jim'll Fix It* is only a small, though important, part of his life. If he wanted day-to-day control of the show's preparation, it would greatly interfere with his advisory, hospital and charity work. For one thing you never know where Jim is going to be next and I would not fancy the job of trying to track him down each day in John O'Groats, Aberdare or wherever.

The most-requested person, the ageless Cliff Richard.

Q: WHAT ARE THE MOST FREQUENT REQUESTS?

At any given time the most frequent Fix-It plea is from teenage females begging, Please, Please, Please, Please, Please to meet the latest pop music craze. When we started in 1975 it was the Osmonds; at the time of writing it is still (just) New Kids on the Block.

Hardly anyone puts the date on their letters nowadays, so if a future historian wanted to discover the year in which an imaginary pile of old Fix-It letters was written, he would need only to see which pop heroes were being requested. We have seen them arrive and we have seen them depart: the Bay City Rollers, Abba, Madness, Duran Duran, Culture Club, Wham, A-ha, New Kids on the Block (well in the case of the New Kids, we have only seen them arrive!); but in all the changing world of pop one person stays on and on. By far the most requested person over all our seventeen years in business has been the timeless Cliff Richard.

The mums love him, the young daughters love him. Some letters even say, "My gran is a fan, so is my mum and so am I." And when Cliff has appeared on the programme he has always done us proud. He once effected a reunion with the Shadows. In the special tenth anniversary programme in 1985 he sprang a lovely surprise on one of the mum generation when her daughter (also a fan) brought Cliff home with her to sing a song for mum in their front room.

In that same anniversary show we tried to reflect two of the other most oft-repeated requests:

Swimming with a dolphin: On this occasion we managed to get a whole school of dolphins to swim with a school of children.

Walking down a grand staircase in a ballgown: A very frequent request from ladies of a certain age, who for some reason think their request is unique. ("You'll probably think I'm mad, Jim, but . . .") In our studio recording, ten ladies in ten "sticky-out" ballgowns walked down the grandest staircase we could fit into the television studio. They were greeted by the ten most handsome partners we could find for them.

Other perennials are things to do with horses, things to do with ballet, things to do with aeroplanes and things to do with football (although football requests are markedly on the decline). I should add that three times as many letters come from females as from males and the best ideas tend to come from females. This is reflected in the programmes, where there is always a shortage of men and boys.

Q: WHAT IS THE MOST DIFFICULT THING YOU HAVE HAD TO FIX?

Fourteen-year-old Catriona Nisbett's Fix-It letter was a tall order: "Please can you fix it for me to be an ambassador for a day?"

I hardly dared telephone the Foreign Office but, when I spoke to their press officer, he took me seriously and was most helpful. At our preliminary discussion we said we wanted Catriona to have the toughest assignment and asked if Moscow might be a possible placement for our young ambassador. This was in 1985 before the start of the East-West thaw and it was asking a lot. However, our man in Moscow, Sir Bryan Cartledge, was approached and he gave an okay as far as he was concerned. Our request to pursue the project went right up the line

"Dear Jim," wrote six-year-old Kristofer, "I love dynamite, but my mum said I couldn't have any for Christmas. So please can you fix it for me to blow something up."

How about an old block of flats in Leeds?

3 – 2 – 1 – BANG!

"My lords, ladies and gentlemen,"... a trainee MC.

to the Foreign Secretary, Sir Geoffrey Howe. He not only gave his assent, but said that when Catriona came back from her "posting", she should follow the correct ambassadorial procedure and make a report to him personally. We were to be allowed to film this debriefing.

For reasons of economy when we film overseas we usually work with a local film crew. I made the mistake of asking if it would be possible for us to work with a Russian crew while we were in Moscow and got the reply: "Are you mad? A Russian film crew in the British embassy? They'd love that and we're certainly not going to fix it for them!"

We had the go-ahead from the Foreign Office, but there was still the hurdle of approval from Moscow to be cleared. The authorities there were very dubious about what we were up to, suspecting, I think, that we would be trying to disseminate anti-Soviet propaganda. It was hard enough trying to explain to them what *Jim'll Fix It* was. The phone-calls which researcher Jeremy Geelan made sorting out the details must have added up to a week of phone-time. With an enormous amount of help from the British embassy and the BBC's man in Moscow we were finally given permission to go ahead. But one week later a new problem arose.

The British government decided to expel some senior Soviet diplomats on charges of spying. As always Moscow immediately reciprocated by repatriating the same number of British diplomats in what the papers called a "tit-for-tat" expulsion. Our Moscow embassy was therefore severely understaffed and in no mood to play *Jim'll Fix It*. The project,

"Well, that's fixed that," says Kristofer.

for the time being, was cancelled.

The following year, with a slightly improved diplomatic climate, we started all over again and this time we were successful. The Russian authorities took us much more seriously than they needed to. A KGB heavy, whom we called Mr Nyet, accompanied us everywhere and I know that our telephones were bugged.

The people at our embassy did a great job. Our ambassador, Sir Bryan, graciously made himself scarce. "While Catriona is here, she is the ambassador," he said. "She may have the use of my Rolls Royce and the car may fly my Union Flag." (Only the ambassador is allowed to do so.)

The members of "her" staff stood up respectfully when Catriona entered the room for their meeting and delivered their reports to her, exactly as they would to the real ambassador. Her gleaming chauffeur-driven Rolls stood out like an extremely elegant thumb among the Ladas as she drove past the Kremlin on her way to visit a political reception at the Orwellian-sounding House of Friendship, a British trade fair, a rather surprising pop concert given by the Nolan sisters and a one-to-one meeting with the American ambassador in his embassy. One of my favourite double-takes was that done by the Russian soldier on guard outside the United States embassy. As the

Philippa launches a ship. The bottle broke on the sixth attempt and the new vessel slipped sideways into the narrow river. (An additional Fix-It for local anglers was that the huge wave created by the launch stranded hundreds of fish in the field opposite.)

ambassadorial Roller rolled into the driveway, he sprang to attention and "presented" his Kalashnikov in salute. Then he looked into the car and saw, not the British ambassador, but a fourteen-year-old young lady looking as cool as a cucumber and giving him a regal nod.

Sir Geoffrey Howe came to the studio and presented Catriona with her "Jim Fixed It For Me" badge. It had certainly all been worth the effort.

Q: HOW MANY LETTERS DO YOU GET?

In the early days of the programme I was occasionally asked this question by journalists. It was something I would have liked to know the answer to myself, but at first I had no idea how to go about it. I certainly was not going to count them. Then – probably for the only time in my life – I was able to say that my university education was of use to me in my job as a television producer. As part of my economics course I studied statistics and our lecturer in that subject was always keen to stress the importance of a "sample survey". The essence of a sample survey is that, if you investigate a genuinely random small sample of a large group, your findings will be the same as if you had investigated the whole group. If you find the average shoe size of a group of two hundred five-year-olds, you will have the average shoe size of all the five-year-olds in the country. How did we do that with mailbags of letters?

The great majority of our mail comes

Rolf Harris demonstrates didgeridoos and don'ts. Breathing exercises include breathing in through the nose while spitting out water.

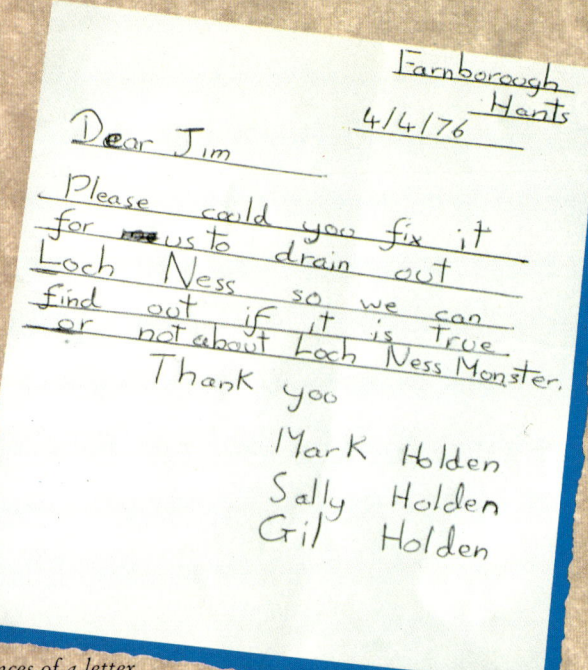

The chances of a letter being "fixed" are about five thousand to one.

during that part of the year when the programme is on the air. Not unreasonably, occasional viewers of television programmes assume that, when a series is currently on the air, it is going to be on every week of the year and that, when it is off the air, it is never going to be on again. I decided first to find the average weight of a bulging mailbag. The canteen staff at the BBC Television Centre kindly let us use their scales. Having lugged the first sack all the way from our office to the kitchen, I concluded that ten sacks would be enough for our sample. Their average weight was forty-one pounds. Then we sampled the average number of letters to the pound, a surprisingly large number, it turned out: sixty-two letters to the pound. (If every letter had been the maximum permitted weight, there would have been only eight letters to the pound.) Over a period of two weeks we received ten mailbags and the series runs for fourteen weeks. Thus:

14 weeks × 10 mailbags × 41 pounds × 62 letters = **355,880 letters.**

So – in a carefully prepared statement – I said that we receive three hundred and fifty thousand letters a year. And I challenge anyone to disprove it.

Q: DO YOU READ ALL THE LETTERS?

Having established a mountain of three hundred and fifty thousand letters, what do you do next? It is not really satisfactory to farm out the preliminary reading of them to readers who have no working knowledge of the programme. Whoever is going to do that first sorting needs to know what requests have already been "fixed" in past programmes and what the show is looking for in its present series. The best-suited readers are therefore the members of the production team. So, whenever there is a lull in other activities in the *Jim'll Fix It* office, the cry goes up, "Read some letters."

These arrive in the office already partly processed. They have been opened (but not read) by other BBC staff members, who volunteer for the work to earn a bit of overtime at home. Their job is to separate the letters from their envelopes, chuck away the envelopes and attach letters to their enclosures, such as photographs, audio and video cassettes and (surprisingly often) the manuscripts of books, which the hopeful authors want Jim to get published. The other duty is to send a standard acknowledgment to those writers who enclose a stamped, addressed envelope.

If the next stage of processing the letters was left to the production team, however, they would not get through them all in time and we do want to be able to stick by our guarantee that all our mail does get read. So there is some farming out to selected readers with a knowledge of the programme. Chief among these is

When the Prime Minister was a Jim (Callaghan) and the President of the USA a Jimmy (Carter), the tabloids could not resist the puns.

my wife, Susie, who works at home as a freelance researcher at those times when our five-year-old daughter, Lulu, is at school or in bed. Susie knows what the programme is capable of and what we are looking for. She also has a mental list of the Fix-Its we have already done going back over many years. When opportunities arise, such as the imminent arrival of

My wife, Susie, looking for pearls. She gets through the already-opened letters at a fair rate and can read "New Kids on the Block" and "Liverpool Football Club" at fifty yards.

a popular singer into the country, I can call her from the office and say, "Start putting [e.g.] Jason Donovan letters to one side; we may be able to get him on the programme." If we are successful and manage to book the star or band of the moment, there will be a lucky dip to see who gets to meet their heroes.

It has been suggested that we could make life a lot easier for ourselves if, like many other television programmes, we used the words "on a postcard, please", but I think we would lose a lot if we did so. An important part of the atmosphere of the programme is the showing on the screen of our contributors' letters, which can ramble in an intimate and charming

way. Postcards have to be short and to the point and, being more public, they tend to inhibit the writer.

I think almost any address will reach us, even if the stamp is stuck on with Sellotape.

Q: ARE PEOPLE CO-OPERATIVE?

Once the programme got off the ground, offers of assistance started to flood in from companies and organisations who had something which – for one reason or another – they wanted to be seen on television. Any public relations person worth their salt (and many are not) should be able to see the massive publicity opportunity that exists in lending their client's hotel, football team or hot air balloon to a TV show whose audience size runs into eight figures. However, there have been offers which have been purely philanthropic, such as the Swiss millionaire, who – without asking for any kind of publicity in return – financed the "rescue" of a young boy whose dream was to be saved by a St Bernard mountain dog from the Alpine snows. Our anonymous benefactor had said simply that he liked the idea of the programme and was glad to be able to help.

I think it is because of Jimmy Savile's renowned charity work that a lot of people are so helpful when we ask them to take part in a Fix-It. It is perhaps a way of showing their appreciation. From the earliest days we have managed to secure the services of the famous and the influential.

At the time of our first series, Morecambe and Wise were probably at the peak of their enormous popularity. A young girl had written to us complaining how unfair it was that it was always Eric Morecambe who slapped Ernie Wise's cheeks and never the other way round. She wanted to redress the balance by giving Eric a smack. The two comedy stars agreed to take part, which was particularly brave of Eric Morecambe. The "stage slap", which he used to administer to Ernie Wise, was done with the fingers only, which after the smack were immediately withdrawn again. Even a nine-year-old can deliver a fair whack with the flat of the hand and, when this young lady delivered her slap, the look of anguish on Eric's face was not feigned.

Morecambe and Wise were the tops and if any other celebrities were in doubt, from now on it was clear that to appear on *Jim'll Fix It* was okay. In 1976 Muhammad Ali made a memorable appearance, chatting to a group of eager fans. Jimmy brought the interview to an unusual close by proffering his chin to the champ and asking to be struck on the jaw. Muhammad Ali replied, "And who will be your beneficiarary [sic]?"

Another interview in the same year was with the Leader of the Opposition, Margaret Thatcher, answering the questions of four enthusiastic youngsters in her House of Commons office. As she awarded the Fix-It badges she asked Jimmy Savile, "When are you going to fix it for me to get the key to Number Ten?" and complained that our ribbons were rather a socialist red. Three years later, when she became Prime Minister, we sent her a "Jim Fixed It For Me" medallion with a blue ribbon. That act was not broadcast, for it might have been taken as a transgression of the BBC's code of political impartiality.

We achieved a political balance soon after the Mrs Thatcher Fix-It. We approached the Chancellor of the Exchequer, Denis Healey, following up a request to find out what was inside the famous, tattered Budget Day briefcase. Maybe the fact that the Leader of the Opposition had already made an appearance encouraged the Chancellor to say "yes". After a serious question-and-answer session a twinkling Mr Healey opened the box to reveal to his interviewers hundreds of gold coins – or rather, chocolate coins wrapped in gold foil. So now we know.

John Betjeman, the Poet Laureate, came to the studio to meet some aspiring

Almost any address will do, even if the stamp has been sellotaped on.

young poets. Jimmy Savile declared himself to be a writer of poetry and offered Sir John a sample:

> Roses are red,
> Violets are grey,
> Got the wrong colour,
> Never mind, ay?

to the utter chortling delight of the Poet Laureate.

Young Joanne Knowles from Grays, Essex was worried about the language problems encountered by Manuel from *Fawlty Towers*. She wanted to give him some English lessons. Manuel, alias Andrew Sachs, eagerly accepted Joanne's offer. I had to write to John Cleese asking his permission to use the *Fawlty Towers* copyright. I had known John during our early days in BBC Radio together. He had found my name somehow comical and had used it occasionally for a character in the London Weekend Television comedy programme *At Last the 1948 Show* (broadcast, I hasten to add, in 1967). In my letter to John I said that since he had used my name in the past, I hoped he would let me use his creation. He replied saying that we could certainly use *Fawlty Towers* for our Fix-It, but that in fact it had been a totally different Roger Ordish whose name he had borrowed for his programme.

A blind woman, who lived in Edward Heath's constituency, sent him a tape recording. Sybil Howlett's cassette was both a spoken letter and a piece of music which she had composed herself and recorded on an electronic organ. She asked the ex-premier if he knew of any way in which she could get to hear her composition being played by an orchestra. Mr Heath sent the letter on to Jimmy Savile and that gave us the opportunity to bargain. We would get the music arranged for orchestra and hire an orchestra if Mr Heath would come and conduct the piece on our programme. He agreed, and as Sybil sat and heard her composition played by a large orchestra conducted by a former Prime Minister, tears rolled down her cheeks from her sightless eyes.

Not long after the transmission of this event Sybil remarkably regained some ability to see. She told us about it and we were able to do a second Fix-It for her. She had just enough sight to be able to ride a motorbike (not on the public highway). All this was too much for the *Daily Star*, who on December 22nd, 1982 gave the story their front page headline:

"JIM FIXES A MIRACLE"

It helped the programme gain a massive nineteen million viewers on Christmas Day, the top figure for BBC or ITV during the Christmas period. The co-operation we get certainly rewards us and, I hope, those who so kindly co-operate.

"Breakfast for one, please," asked Joanne on her visit to Fawlty Towers.

"Breakfast for Juan?" enquired Manuel. "Where is Juan?"

DAILY STAR

...MBER 22, 1982   15p (16p CIs)   Printed in London

STAR CHRISTMAS EXCLUSIVE

Just watch me go... Sybil rides again on Jim's show

...00 bill to Scargill

By GEORGE HILL

...rthur Scargill was cleared of... And it will cost his union ...ick up most of his legal bill after...

Happy... Mr. Scargill yesterday

Jimmy... he was very impressed

JIM FIXES A MIRACLE

Gran Sybil to see the TV show that made us all weep

MILLIONS of TV viewers will share the Christmas miracle that Jimmy Savile fixed for great-granny Sybil Howlett.

Two years ago the nation wept with her as blind Sybil listened to former Premier

By BARRY GARDNER

Edward Heath conducting the moving piece of music she had composed.

Now, on Christmas Day, Sybil, 71, will see the concert herself because she has partially regained her sight.

Q: ARE PEOPLE UNCO-OPERATIVE?

Very seldom, but when they do not want to help, they usually give one of two standard replies:

A: We should love to do this, but unfortunately our insurance does not allow us to . . .

B: If we let one person do it, they will all want to.

Let me give you an example of a B, which happened within the BBC's own Television Centre. Back in 1975, as they do now, the corporation used the working newsroom as a background for the newsreader. It was more clearly visible then than it is now and you could see working newsfolk at their desks behind the reader, answering phones and typing reports. Occasionally a busy messenger could be seen scurrying across the office with a news story freshly torn from the teleprinter. All old stuff now, but as far as Gwen Charlton from Morpeth, Northumbria was concerned all this activity was much more interesting than the news itself and she hit upon a most original idea. "Please could you fix it for me to ride a white horse through the back of the newsroom, while Richard Baker is reading the news?"

Well, not during the real news we couldn't, but Richard Baker agreed to read some special news just for our programme and the man in charge of BBC TV news gave us his assent. The trouble was that the newsroom was on the sixth floor of the Television Centre and the house manager of the building, the man responsible for the bricks and mortar of the centre, was a "no" man.

"The weight of a horse's hoof per square inch would exceed the safety loading limits of my floors."

I offered to have boards laid down to spread the load.

"What if the horse makes a mess on my floors?"

I offered to have tarpaulins laid and to clean up any muck myself.

For a moment he was cornered, but then he remembered standard reply B, above. "If I let you do it, they'll all want to do it."

"NO THEY WON'T, DAVID," I replied vociferously.

I think in his troubled mind he was picturing hordes of zebras, camels and rhinoceroses, all queueing to get into his nice, clean newsroom. However, I have to say in the house manager's favour that he did at last give in and we were able to stage our own little news story:

"Gwen Charlton from Morpeth, Northumbria, is missing. She was last seen riding a white horse in the region of the BBC's Television Centre in London."

Enter Gwen, weaving her way between the desks on Snowball.

The effect was delightful.

I managed to obtain from the Distillers Company a large poster advertising a whisky with a slogan that was well known at the time. I sent it to the house manager's office. It said: "You can take a white horse anywhere."

(Illustration of White Horse poster, by permission, United Distillers.)

Q: DO YOU HAVE AN AGE LIMIT?

I hope not. Our youngest ever Fixee was two years old. His parents had just had the thrill of hearing him speak for the first time. His was an unusual first utterance. The words were "JCB." Some construc-

"If we let one person do it, they'll all want to."

tion work was in progress right next to their house and their little boy was enchanted by the versatile digging machines of that name. Despite her son's limited vocabulary it was clear to his mother that a ride on a JCB would be little John's greatest dream. Jim was asked to fix it and did.

JCB is a remarkable and dynamic British company bearing the name of its founder, J.C. Bamforth. They have a keen eye for publicity and were only too pleased to let the two-year-old be guest of honour at a display by their special formation team of mechanical diggers. With split-second accuracy the team's drivers perform a spectacular musical ride to the sound of canned Sousa marches. As the climax to the show two lines of JCBs with their buckets raised face each other, touching bucket to bucket, and then inch carefully forward. This causes all the front wheels to rise off the ground, forming an avenue of earth-movers looking like the guard of honour at a military wedding. Through this tunnel came the JCB-in-chief. As the martial music came to an end the driver brought his machine to a halt in front of the dais where sat little John and his mum. The driver solemnly stood to attention at his controls and saluted our youngest Fixee, who gurgled his appreciation and said, "JCB," again.

Our senior Fixee was a hundred and one years older than little John. This is how Jimmy Savile introduced him to the

The Dancing Diggers Display Team.

viewers: "My next guest did not fight in the First World War, the reason being that he was too old."

The delightful one-hundred-and-three-year-old James had been a professional gardener (a lot of gardeners seem to live to a ripe old age) and his Fix-It was to go for a ride in a racing car. We filmed him standing by the track, looking frail but alert in his best Sunday suit, while his host, a burly Australian racing-driver, explained what was in store for him.

"Well, James, we've managed to find you a two-seater. We shall be taking you round the circuit at high speed in this twelve-litre Maserati."

The old man's reply became a catchphrase in our office for years to come: "Ooh, I shall anticipate that."

Expressing his appreciation to Jimmy Savile in the studio afterwards, he said, "I have had more fun these last three years than I did in the previous hundred."

Q: ARE THERE ANY FIX-ITS YOU HAVEN'T BEEN ABLE TO DO?

Naturally there have been some pretty weird requests, which we would not dream of attempting such as:

Can you fix it for me to go to the moon?

Please fix it for me to be a Page Three Girl. (See enclosed photos.)

Can you lend me £100,000 until next month?

Please have my ex-boyfriend beaten up.

However, if we are talking about things that we set up to be fixed, and then failed, we have a pretty good record. It is said in show business, "Never work with animals or children." *Jim'll Fix It*

Role reversal. A seven-year-old Father Christmas wanted to bring tidings of comfort and joy to the old folk.

It was like that scene from An Officer and a Gentleman *when Lionel Blair went to surprise factory supervisor Gwynneth Fitzgerald at her place of work. A week later they were in the studio, tapping to "Lullaby of Broadway".*

frequently tries both and it was in this department that we once came unstuck. There was a young lady who wanted to ride on the back of a giant tortoise and her wish was all ready to be granted in the television studio. The young lady was perfectly willing, but suddenly the giant tortoise was not. It scuttled surprisingly swiftly off the studio set and the four tough stage crew and handlers who went after it were quite incapable of persuading it to go back on stage. All that the cameras were capable of seeing were the trousered hindquarters of four human beings and barely a glimpse of tortoise. We had to abandon the project and own up that the only thing which has foiled *Jim'll Fix It* has been a tortoise.

For the record, since then Jim has fixed a ride on a giant tortoise as part of Victoria Mountstephan's *Holiday Programme* Fix-It in the Seychelles in 1982. She sat on the back of Esmeralda, who is claimed to be the world's oldest living animal.

Q: WHAT ARE THE CHANCES OF A REQUEST BEING FIXED?

There are fourteen programmes made each year and typically in each programme there are three items which have already been filmed on location and two Fix-Its which take place in front of our studio audience. Five times fourteen makes seventy Fixees a year.

$$\frac{350{,}000 \text{ letters}}{70 \text{ Fix-Its}} = 5{,}000\text{-}1$$

That must be approximately the same as the annual chance of winning a prize from one Premium Bond. If you buy more Premium Bonds, you increase your chances of winning. If you write more letters to *Jim'll Fix It*, you do not increase your chances of being fixed, unless in each letter you ask for a different thing.

I must apologise to those parents

whose children are asking, "Will Jim have got my letter yet?" and "When am I going to hear from him?" If it is any comfort, it might be worth reminding them that they do not get a letter from Lytham St Anne's each month saying, "Unfortunately this month your Premium Bonds have not been successful."

Q: WHAT IS THE MOST EXPENSIVE FIX-IT YOU HAVE DONE?

It depends on how you look at it, I suppose. There was Karen Doswell, who sat in the studio wearing a tiara and other jewellery valued at a quarter of a million pounds, but then – not surprisingly – she had to hand it all back at the end of the show. Toby Gilette was more fortunate and his Fix-It was, I believe, the most financially rewarding. Being a Toby, he thought he should have a Toby jug in his own likeness and wrote, asking Jim to fix it. We approached the famous china manufacturers, Royal Doulton of Stoke-on-Trent and they offered to make a jug for Toby. They treated the subject with total seriousness, as if it was to be one of their major products and took Toby through the whole process from having an image of his face sculpted in clay to seeing the final glazed character jug emerge from the oven. Doulton's only divergence from normal procedure was that, instead of manufacturing a few thousand jugs in this design, they made only three: the important one for Toby himself, one for their own permanent museum and one for Jimmy Savile to auction for charity.

Character jugs, as they are properly called, are collector's items and when Jimmy's mug was auctioned at Sotheby's, the top bid came by telephone from South Africa and was an unbelievable sixteen thousand pounds (this was in 1985). The news was too much for Toby's family, if only because of the cost of insuring their jug. The next year Toby's jug went at auction for nearly the same amount. So after all that, Toby has not got a Toby jug of himself, but he has got a handy *Jim'll Fix It* nest egg.

Some of our overseas filming can look expensive and is sometimes the cause of a few angry viewers' letters, complaining of extravagance. Generally, however, the foreign trips do not cost any more than filming at home. We do not normally undertake an overseas assignment unless the government tourist office of the place we are visiting can secure cut-price travel and accommodation for all concerned. To keep the number of people travelling to a minimum we work with a local film crew, which can cause language problems, but saves a lot of money. The number of people travelling from Britain is three or four: director, researcher, Fixee plus one parent if Fixee is a child.

The most expensive Fix-It in terms of money spent by the BBC was probably Martha Hillier's. It was fixed for her to roller-skate with the cast of the Andrew Lloyd Webber/Richard Stilgoe musical, *Starlight Express*. This involved taking three camera crews and a lot of lighting equipment into the theatre. We had to pay the actors and the orchestra and a fair amount to the staff of the theatre. Costs of different fixes vary enormously but they balance out and (touch wood) we stay within our modest budget. We are much cheaper than most entertainment shows on television. As a footnote to the *Starlight Express* Fix-It: when Andrew Lloyd Webber came to the studio to give Martha her badge, he invited Martha and her mother to fly to New York and see the opening night of the musical on Broadway. I need hardly add that Andrew Lloyd Webber paid for the trip.

Toby Gilette takes his likeness in china-clay out of the oven. He did not know then there was to be a £16,000 price-tag on his head.

63

What might have looked to the casual observer like the biggest waste of money was when a young lady called Rebecca took a gas poker in her hand and set fire to six million pounds' worth of banknotes. In fact these notes had ceased to have any value. Rebecca was at the Bank of England's special furnaces, the graveyard of those dirty fivers that you see bank clerks pull out of the wad. Rebecca's mother had written to say that money would never burn a hole in her daughter's pocket and could Rebecca have the chance to burn a hole in some money instead – six million pounds in all.

At the end of it all Jimmy Savile expressed great horror that the whole of a disc-jockey's weekly wage should be allowed to go up in smoke like that.

The most expensive Fix-It in terms of money-not-for-burning must be the case of a ten-year-old boy whom we temporarily called Admiral Peter Macleod. He was given nominal command of a NATO naval exercise back in 1975. Twenty-odd warships (including an aircraft carrier and a nuclear submarine), a couple of squadrons of naval fighters and a handful of helicopters were his to play with for a morning.

The price he had to pay was being winched from one of his vessels to another while travelling at sea. It is not easy to estimate the real cost of all that but it could certainly run to a pound-sign followed by seven figures!

Money to burn: BEFORE

WHAT, WHERE AND WHEN?

Money to burn: DURING and AFTER

"Admiral" Peter Macleod changes horses midstream.

65

Q: DOES JIMMY SAVILE GO OUT FILMING WITH YOU?

Only on special occasions, when the request involves him specifically. One of the reasons why he does not come to our locations is the very practical one that with his busy schedule of other commitments, it would be extremely tricky to sort out a timetable whereby Jim, the Fixee and the event concerned would all be available on the same day. However the important reason is that the filming day is the Fixee's big day. He or she is the star and, if Jimmy were there, he would draw a lot of the public attention and that would tend to push the star-for-a-day into second place. But whenever Jim does come filming with us, some hilarious moments are almost guaranteed.

In 1975 with Jimmy Savile on a visit to Israel, it was the perfect opportunity for us to fix it for young Gary Merrie, from the Salvation Army's famous Strawberry Field, Liverpool, to have a conducted tour of the birthplace of Jesus as part of our first ever Christmas programme. Our Israeli camera crew was trying to take a peaceful shot of Jim and young Gary walking towards Manger Square in Bethlehem. Each time we tried for the shot a car would come between the camera and its subject. I think we had reached take seven when finally we seemed to be getting the perfect picture. At the last second, round the corner came hurtling a large pink Cadillac, driven by a demonstrative Arabic gentleman blasting on the car's horn. By way of comment I turned to the film crew and, trying my impression of Sylvester the Cat, shouted, "aah shuddup!"

Unfortunately the driver heard me, reversed his Cadillac back up the hill and enquired of the assembled company, "Who say 'shut up'?" then turned his gaze on me, the tall pink-faced Englishman. My first thought was that I would now probably go down in history as the man who was the immediate cause of the Third World War.

Our Israeli cameraman leapt into the breach and said, "He was saying 'shut up' to me," but this explanation did not convince the Cadillac-driver at all.

He pointed a wagging finger at me and said, "No. It is to me he say 'shut up'. And I say to you. I say . . ."

Here he paused for a moment, presumably so that he could choose his

Typically in a day's filming the Jim'll Fix It *crew creates between five and ten minutes' finished screen time. (This compares with a daily productivity of about three minutes for a television drama, one to two minutes for a feature film and ten to fifteen seconds for a TV commercial.)*

> Dear Jimmy Saville.
> I would like to serve the Queen her dinner in my brownie uniform. When I was enrolled as a brownie I promised to serve the Queen. Please make this possible for me.
> Love from
> Victoria Armitstead.
> (Age 7).

words carefully. I was awaiting one of those classical Arabic curses involving the offspring of infidel dogs and so forth, but he finally said, still wagging the finger, "To me you say 'shut up'. To you I say *one hundred shut ups*!" and screeched off in his Cadillac, nought to sixty in eight seconds.

Jimmy Savile, who had just been able to suppress his mirth during all of the above, came over to me and said with mock solemnity, "Henceforth this street shall be known as the Street of the One Hundred Shut-ups."

Q: DO YOU GIVE YOUR POSTAGE STAMPS TO CHARITY?

No, unless the people who open the letters are prepared to separate the stamps from the envelopes in their own free time. It would be quite wrong for the BBC to shell out pounds in pay-packets so that a few pence could go to a charity. The average price for current British postage stamps is seventy-five pence a kilo and it takes an awful lot of stamps to make a kilo.

Q: IS IT HARD TO KEEP YOUR SURPRISES SECRET?

My advice is only tell people secrets on what MI5 calls a "need-to-know" basis. In our experience where secrets fail is when surprise Fixee's wife tells friend B, who tells her friend C, who does not know it is meant to be a surprise. C then goes to surprise Fixee and says, "I hear you're going on *Jim'll Fix It*," which he isn't, because if the secret is blown and we know about it we abandon the project. Fortunately that has happened only twice in seventeen years.

We nearly blew the secret when we had organised a surprise coach and four to take a bride to the church. To film in a public place we have to get permission from the police. On this occasion the inspector told the PC and the PC plodded up the path to Number 43, knocked on the door and enquired, "Is this the house where they're doing the *Jim'll Fix It*?"

Luckily it was the mother of the bride who answered the door and she marched the constable backwards down the path with her hand firmly over his mouth.

Probably the hardest secret we have ever had to keep was when we had to get the hottest pop music property of the moment into the assembly hall of a school without any of the pupils finding out about it. Three fifth-formers had written to Jim complaining about the badly played Brahms they had to endure at assembly and asking for something a bit more up to date. The headmaster was a good sport. It may sound ridiculous, but we treat these surprises like the hottest military intelligence. I would not tell the head what I wanted to see him about – just that I wanted to see him. He let me visit him. It was decided that only the assistant headmaster and one caretaker needed to be told. The logistics of how to smuggle the band in and where to hide them were efficiently organised but the biggest stumbling block was how to explain to a rock band that there was such a thing as five o'clock in the morning; however they turned up on time. Perhaps they had not been to bed.

By the time the keenest pupils and staff started to arrive the musicians were safely hidden behind the assembly hall stage. At nine o'clock the deputy headmaster addressed the school from in front of the closed stage curtains. The unexplained camera crew seemed hardly to interest the six hundred sophisticated pupils. "We encourage you," said the deputy head to

WHAT, WHERE AND WHEN?

Filming on a tea plantation in Sri Lanka, I tried delicately to suggest to the manager that our film would look better if it featured the younger female tea-pickers. He immediately called up his foreman and shouted down the phone: "For the filming tomorrow we require only beautiful pluckers!"

Simon makes Jimmy Savile a cup of tea – from scratch.

69

the school, "to let us hear your comments and criticisms of our activities. But three of you have taken things one stage further and written to the media. I refer to Christine Broad, Kate Christadoulou and Sharon Cobren."

The camera was on this trio as they looked at each other in total bewilderment. Then the deputy head read out their letter and all became clear.

He went on: "So here for Christine, Kate and Sharon are Boy George and Culture Club!" and up went the curtain.

The girls roared with laughter, the school cheered and the band sang. A total and most satisfactory surprise.

Q: DO YOU GET OFFERED OPPORTUNITIES WHICH YOU CANNOT TAKE?

Public relations consultants frequently offer us hot air balloons. We get plenty of requests for hot air balloons, but the ones on offer are usually covered in unsuitable advertising, as are most racing cars, another frequent offer. (Although I do not quite know what we are expected to fix in single-seat racing cars.)

We get great assistance from the armed forces and there is usually no problem matching what they can offer to letters to the programme. Once, however, the Royal Air Force asked us if we had any letters asking to have a go at aerial photography and I could not lay my hands on such a request. None the less, we wanted to take up the RAF's offer since it would make an interesting film. With a bit of lateral thinking we hit upon the idea of using a letter which simply asked Jimmy Savile for a signed photograph. There are plenty of these. It was just a matter of finding a suitable candidate. Fourteen-year-old Dawn Ross from Ruskington, Lincolnshire was approached. She could have a signed photograph, she was told, but she would have to take the picture herself. Jimmy Savile would not be in a photographic studio; he would be on the deck of a ferry between Jersey and Weymouth. So to get her picture Dawn would have to fly low past him in a Royal Air Force maritime patrol aircraft and take a picture of him from it. Contrived? Certainly, but young Dawn accepted the challenge.

The aircraft in question was a Hawker Siddeley Nimrod, developed from the famous Comet airliner and designed to seek out enemy submarines. It carries a crew of twelve and more electronic equipment than a television studio. Despite that, there was still room for Dawn and the film crew.

One cold December morning, as Jimmy Savile was leaving Jersey on the ferry, Dawn was at the crew briefing at RAF St Mawgan in Cornwall. Flight Lieutenant Paul Ingoe addressed his crew: "Our object this morning is to locate Jimmy Savile on the Channel Island ferry as she heads for Weymouth. The vessel should be in clear waters here on the map at approximately thirteen hundred hours. We shall approach to starboard from a southerly direction, height seventy-six metres, speed two hundred knots. Having received instruc-

QUESTION: *What has Jim fixed here? (See next page for answer)*

ANSWER: (from previous page) ... a chance to play the alpenhorn

tion, Miss Ross will take the photographs."

Take-off was on time. An eagle-eyed aero-spotter might have noticed something unusual about this aircraft. In the middle of the huge RAF "roundel" was a *Jim'll Fix It* sticker.

The Nimrod flew low over the Cornish cliffs, banking at nearly ninety degrees, then climbed steeply to its cruising altitude. Once at ten thousand feet Dawn was given a swift lesson in aerial photography. In the midst of all this advanced technology the procedure seemed a bit straightforward. The photographer holds the camera by hand, opens a window, points the camera at the subject and presses a button.

"Don't put the camera outside the window, though. Remember there's a two-hundred-and-fifty-mile-an-hour wind out there. That's how fast we shall be travelling." At that speed there is very little time to line up on the subject. Having dived down to two hundred and fifty feet above sea level, the aircraft did one dummy run and then went round again for the take.

When an aircraft flies low over the sea, it is travelling through air as turbulent as the waves immediately beneath it. Dawn said quietly, "I think I am going to be sick," and was. She threw up, but she did not give up.

After a couple of minutes a voice shouted, "We are going to open the window; it will be very noisy."

With slightly trembling hands Dawn picked up the camera and pointed. A voice counted down the seconds of the approach, "five, four, three, two, one." Dawn clicked on the "zero" and through the blur was able to see Jimmy Savile waving on the foredeck of the SS *Earl William*.

Dawn's snap was a little out of focus, but Jim's distinctive figure was clearly visible when in the studio he signed his name across it.

I wonder if Dawn ever asked anyone else for their autograph after that.

Q: HAVE YOU EVER DONE ANYTHING DANGEROUS?

We are always very careful not to do anything really dangerous. Every activity involves some degree of danger, but I believe we should not take a risk any greater than that involved in driving a car on a public road.

We have had some fun in the past doing things that looked fairly dangerous, like the case of the young woman who wanted to stand on an aircraft's wing in mid-air. Breathtaking and alarming it certainly was, but since she was securely strapped on she was as safe on the wing as she would have been sitting securely in the seat behind the pilot.

In the summer of 1981 inhabitants of St Ives, Cornwall, who are not easily sur-

prised, raised their eyebrows when they saw a bright red Ford Cortina hurtle along their jetty and go straight off the end into the sea. Hillary Nichols was being "fixed". A young mother with no fewer than five children, she was looking for a challenge other than that of looking after five young children and had decided that nothing would suit her better than driving off the end of a pier. Was it dangerous? Not unreasonably so. The safety precautions for an exercise of this nature were stringent. Stunt director Tim Condren was in charge of the operation and he first supervised the drilling of holes in the old banger we had bought for the job (later to be resold for scrap). The purpose of the holes, Tim explained, was to make the car sink as quickly as possible. The behaviour of a car which goes straight under is more predictable than that of a near-watertight vehicle bobbing about on the surface for a few minutes. Ballast was added to the vehicle to encourage it to nose-dive rather than make a spiralling entry into the sea. Tim tested Hillary's ability to swim underwater and gave her lessons in using the breathing apparatus at the depth she would reach when the car hit the bottom. Aircraft-style safety harnesses were attached, Hillary had a test-drive on dry land and then she was ready to go.

Tim gave a signal to his two stuntmen/divers, who dropped off the end of the jetty to be on standby underwater, in case any unforeseen emergency should arise. Two cameras were ready to film the event, one at the end of the jetty and the other on the inshore lifeboat, kindly lent to us for the occasion. There was a big crowd of onlookers and it was well known that we would be doing the stunt at five minutes to four, at which time the tide would be at its optimum height.

Then there was a snag. At six minutes to four an anonymous and mentally deranged person, presumably with a grudge against us or against the world in general, made a hoax distress call for the lifeboat. Our waterborne film crew had to evacuate the lifeboat as quickly as possible and luckily a neighbouring fisherman generously lent us his boat as a substitute. But due to the hoax call we were running a few minutes late for the most suitable height of tide and maybe that is why things did not go exactly as planned. On the other hand it could have been that Hillary drove the car a little bit faster than she had been told to. The Cortina hit the water square on and started to sink quickly, but once under water it slowly continued its forward roll and in the end landed in the sand on its roof. Tim Condren, now upside down in the passenger

No going back. Hillary's Cortina at the point of impact.

seat, could still just see his driver through the murky water. She had correctly inserted the breathing apparatus in her mouth, she had undone her safety harness and was calmly feeling for the door handle.

To us on the jetty it felt like an age before the driver and passenger rose to the surface again. In fact there had been thirty-seven seconds between the car hitting the water and the re-emergence of Hillary and Tim. Hillary snatched the breathing-tube out of her mouth and shouted, "Can we do it again, please?"

(Safety footnote: A large mobile crane immediately winched the car out of the sea again.)

For me the greatest sense of danger came during our James Bond Fix-It. We were at the old Brooklands airfield near Weybridge in Surrey and the Fix was a meeting with the boffin from the Bond films, Q, alias the delightful actor Desmond Llewelyn. With good publicity in mind the film company had lent us a selection of the props which Bond had received from Q in previous movies, and Lotus cars had provided their latest model, as featured in *The Spy Who Loved Me*. We were filming our young Bond, standing by the door of the Lotus, receiving instructions on the use of his homing-bleep from Q, when a young man came over and asked for a word with me.

"You're remaking that scene from *The Spy Who Loved Me*, aren't you?" he said.

World War II veterans Jack Marsh and Ronald Lappage re-enact their Normandy Landing, courtesy of the Royal Marines.

A miniature addition to Status Quo.

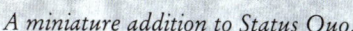

"Please can I marshal an aircraft or meet the Liverpool team?" was the request. She did both. On board the aircraft – unbeknown to her – were Matt Busby, Kenny Dalgliesh and the rest.

"Where's the helicopter?"

He had a point. When James Bond drove the Lotus in the scene in question he was being chased by a helicopter – something that was unfortunately beyond the budget for this particular item.

"I've got a helicopter," continued the young man. "Would you like to use it?"

I thanked him, but had to decline, explaining that we could not possibly afford the three hundred pounds an hour or so (that was then the going rate for the hire of a small helicopter).

"No, no," he said, "I'll do it just for the fun of it."

I readily agreed, thinking it was a great idea until he added, "You had better fly with me so that you can tell me what it is you want the helicopter to do."

I looked at this enthused amateur stunt flyer and his tiny machine and wondered just how experienced he was. I decided not to lose face and replied, "Yes, of course I'll come with you," trying to force a keen smile.

The crew had a Citroën Deux Chevaux as a travelling platform for the camera. The car's motorbike springing gives it a smoother ride and therefore a less bumpy picture than you get with traditional motorcar suspension. I first asked the driver of the Lotus to drive at moderate speed in a straight line along the disused runway and then asked the camera-car-driver to drive slightly ahead of and parallel to the Lotus, trying to keep the Lotus between the camera and the helicopter.

Finally, when I was strapped inside the tiny bubble of the helicopter, I asked the pilot to get the Lotus and the camera-car lined up and to make a series of "attacks" on the Lotus. These were very effective, certainly as far as my stomach was concerned. We seemed to pass just inches over the roofs of both cars in a series of swoops and rolls, which deprived me of any sense of what was straight and what was level. But I am here to tell the tale and must thank again that generous pilot for helping us to make a film which we could not otherwise have afforded – and for giving me the white hair which, I was once told, makes me look distinguished.

Q: HOW LONG IS IT BETWEEN A LETTER BEING SELECTED AND A WISH BEING GRANTED?

It varies enormously. The record for the shortest time was twelve hours. In 1979 the pop music flavour of the year was still that long-lived Swedish star group, Abba. The programme had been trying to secure their services for years – so far without success. Then early one evening out of the blue came an offer. If we could get a Fixee to their recording studio in London by the very next morning, they could "Singalonga Abba". We always keep a stand-by random selection of letters for such popular requests, but by chance all our Abba file contained were letters from such distant places as Aberdeen, Belfast, Truro and so forth and none of them with telephone numbers (not that we normally would give any preference to letters carrying telephone numbers). On this rare occasion we needed somebody local to London and the only thing for us to do was to dive into the bags of unread mail, which for ever decorate our office, in the hope of finding an "Abba" letter from someone who could be in London by nine o'clock the following morning. Luckily the group was so popular that the chances of finding such a letter were quite reasonable.

At 8.00 p.m., the whole team was scanning the contents of the mailbags in silence, when Gill, one of the researchers,

cried in triumph, "Here's one! It's from Essex and there's even a telephone number."

Twelve and a half hours later two dazed twelve-year-olds, Claire Doggett and Clair Lindeman, were singing slightly tremulously with Abba, "Thankyou for the Music".

(Incidentally, Gill Stribling-Wright, the researcher who found the letter, is currently head of the light entertainment department at TV South. I guess she just has the knack.)

The record for the longest wait between writing and being fixed was held for a long time by David Moss. In 1979 we got the opportunity to fulfil David's request, which was to have a lesson in funny walks from Max Wall. There was David's letter filed under W.

I telephoned his mother, who sounded a little hesitant and said, "He's twelve now, you know; he was only eight when he wrote in."

I blew on the letter and a small puff of dust rose from it. Upon being asked, however, the young man was as keen as ever for his master-class in "eccentric dancing".

In 1991 David's record was broken by a

Thank you for the Music: thank you for the Fix-It. Clair, Claire and Abba.

To celebrate the fixing of Helen's request, written ten years before, the team had her badge sprayed with artificial cobwebs.

young lady from Shifnal, Shropshire. Ten years earlier she had written this letter to Jimmy Savile:

Dear Jim,

Please will you come to my birthday party on the 6th of March 1981 or 1982 or 1983 or 1984 or 1985 or 1986 . . .

Love from Helen Gronow aged 6¾

At the end of each series, when I cleared out our "possibles" file, I had always kept this letter just in case one year we might be able to use it. Then last year I realised that the letter was ten years old and asked Jimmy Savile if he could keep the date of Helen's seventeenth birthday party free. He was able to do that and it worked a treat. Helen's mother kept the secret perfectly and set up a great party for her daughter.

On the night Helen was totally bemused when there was a late arrival, Sir Jimmy Savile Kt, OBE, accompanied by a film crew. Jim had Helen's 1981 letter in his hand and enquired, "Can I come to your party, please. I've brought my invitation with me, so you have to let me in. I must apologise for being ten years late."

We still have a few Fix-It letters dating right back to our beginnings in 1975. Maybe one day we shall be able to break even Helen's record.

Q: DO YOU EVER DO ANYTHING USEFUL?

I hope there are always some viewers whom we amuse or entertain and that should be classifiable as useful, but there are definitely times when we can inform as well. In our last series, for instance, there were a couple of items which caused a flood of enquiries. Viewers wrote in

Colin Field proving that it is armour, but it is not a suit.

Colin waiting to surprise unwary visitors to the Tower of London.

The helmet was a poor fit as well. Colin decided that the previous wearer had no ears.

asking where they could get a "hair extension" like the one they had seen Anne Marie being fitted with on the programme. And Margaret Booth's motor safari Fix-It in North Wales fired the imaginations of a lot of people who wanted to know how they could do the same thing.

On occasions we have been able, however, to do more than just inform: we have actually added to the fund of human knowledge. Many years ago Colin Field, aged eight, paid a visit to the Tower of London and was particularly attracted to one exhibit whose label stated: "Suit of armour, seventeenth century, probably made for an eight-year-old boy." Being exactly the right age, Colin longed for the opportunity to try the armour on and wrote to us.

The authorities at the Tower of London considered our request carefully. They did not want to risk damaging a three-hundred-year-old antique with an auction value of around forty thousand pounds. At the same time Colin represented a unique research opportunity for them. If he was the right size, they could give the armour its first living inhabitant for three centuries. They had calculated that the suit had been made for someone 119 centimetres tall and Colin, we found out, was 118 centimetres.

The time it took us to set up the experiment was the time it takes a boy to grow a centimetre. But when it came to our filming day, it turned out that the suit of armour was far from a good fit. In fact the experts realised they were dealing with a mixed batch made up from two different suits. Their researches had been advanced by our Fix-It and we left them with the tricky task of finding the missing halves of the two sets from amongst the rest of the Tower's massive collection.

Jimmy Savile's "magic" chair is the brainchild of Professor Kevin Warwick

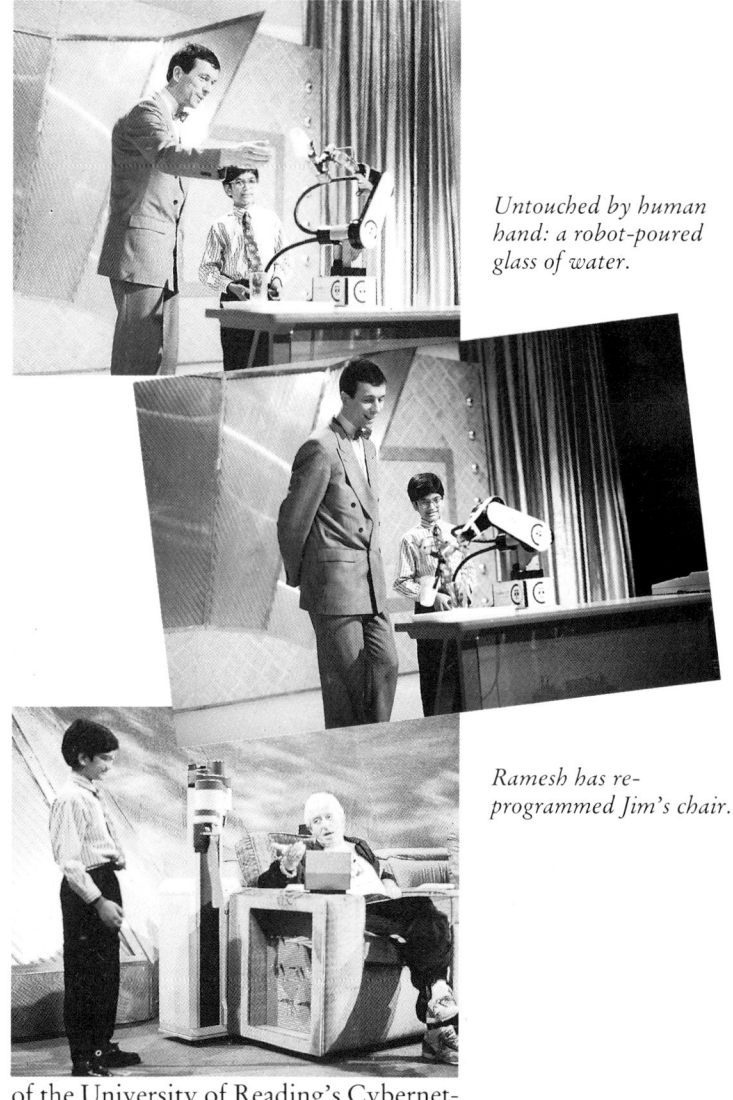

Untouched by human hand: a robot-poured glass of water.

Ramesh has re-programmed Jim's chair.

of the University of Reading's Cybernetics Department. The clever movements of the chair's robotic arm may seem like just a bit of extravagant fun, but they are in fact also serving a serious purpose. The Cybernetics Department is closely linked with Stoke Mandeville Hospital, whose rebuilt spinal unit was funded by Jimmy Savile's ten million pound campaign. It is hoped that experiments with the arm of Jim's chair will help in the development of mechanical aids for Stoke Mandeville's paralysed patients.

Q: HAVE ANY OF YOUR FIX-ITS GONE WRONG?

In making television, as in most things, I suppose, there are minor mishaps all along the way. At the same time I can say that none of our endeavours has backfired on us too seriously. There have been considerable upsets, however, like the following story, in which I shall change the participants' names.

Mr Exec was a businessman whose job took him flying all over the world. His daughter, seven-year-old Daisy Exec, wanted to surprise her daddy and turn up unexpectedly as an air-hostess on one of his flights. The cost and complications of organising a surprise like this on a long-distance international flight would have been prohibitive. However the Execs lived in the Channel Islands and the father had to take a "feeder" airline to London's Heathrow airport before starting his main journey. With these favourable circumstances we were able to set up the stunt with the help of Air UK, who provided Daisy with a perfect scale-model of their stewardess uniform.

One Monday morning at 6.00 a.m., the camera crew was waiting behind a hedge opposite the family's home. At 6.20 we managed to take a candid shot of Mr Exec leaving home and, as soon as his car was out of sight, we dived into the house to film Daisy being dressed in her uniform. We did not have long, but a fast car rushed us to the airport in time for Daisy to board the aircraft and get out of sight

"You 'orrible little boy!" The Guards fix a lesson in "spit and polish" for an untidy recruit.

We fix it for Katy to take part in a Balinese dance in the studio.

behind the curtain which separated the flight-deck from the passenger accommodation. When the plane reached its cruising altitude we went into action.

I have considerable experience of how people react when they are given a pleasant surprise. Actors tend to portray that sensation by gasping, raising their eyebrows, grinning, or clapping their hands and laughing. In real life I find that people's first reaction is more likely to be a sort of rigor mortis of the face, but that is not what Mr Exec did when his little daughter came down the aisle and offered her father some coffee. He gave a big grin and took his little girl in his arms.

"That wasn't a surprise," I murmured to the cameraman. "I wonder how he found out?"

How he found out I discovered later. On the Friday night he had come home and announced to his wife, "I don't need to go to Saudi Arabia until Tuesday now."

His wife's reaction puzzled him. "No, no, you must go on Monday. You have to. I can't explain why."

It was Friday night and she realised that there was no way of getting in contact with the film crew and asking them to postpone everything by twenty-four hours.

"Why do I *have* to go on Monday?"

"I can't tell you why, or it would spoil everything."

Mr Exec was getting suspicious. "What's going on here?"

I do not know the details of the conversation, but I am sure you can imagine them. In the end Mrs Exec had to tell her husband about the *Jim'll Fix It* surprise. All was sweetness and light once more. The couple decided not to tell anyone (including us) about the revelation for the sake of their little girl and the programme.

When a treat is being prepared for someone, there is no telling how they will respond to it. You can lead a horse to water, it is said, but you cannot make it drink. The horse I have in mind is young

When Daniel asked to drive a dog-sledge, had he hoped for a visit to the Arctic wastes? He did it in Lancashire – with a sledge on wheels.

Peter from Leamington. His little cousin had kindly written to Jim on his behalf.

"My cousin is diabetic," she explained, "and we have been looking everywhere for a diabetic chocolate Easter egg for him, but without success. Can you fix one for him, please?"

It was quite a search, but we did manage to get one in the end. Cadbury's did not make them, they told us; try Harrod's. Harrod's told us they no longer sold them, but they gave us the name of a small manufacturer in Sussex who used to supply them. We found the small firm in Sussex, but they said that they did not make them any more. However they kindly offered to make one specially for the programme, a very tricky process, they added.

Two weeks before Easter we were in the studio to record our "Easter Special" and I was confident that we were in possession of Britain's only diabetic chocolate Easter egg. Sitting with Jimmy Savile were little Peter from Leamington, his cousin who had written the letter and "Dr Chocolate", the man who had made the egg for us. The egg was concealed under Jim's glass-topped table and the programme went through its normal procedure: Jim introduced the letter, the girl read it and the picture cut back to Jim,

who asked the apprehensive-looking Dr Chocolate what was so difficult about making Easter eggs out of this special formula chocolate.

At first no sound emerged from the doctor's lips. After about ten seconds there was a faint croaking sound and then he found speech. "Excuse me," he whispered, "I'm so nervous."

Jimmy assured him that there was nothing to worry about and got on with the business of producing the egg. It would not break. He whacked the table with it to the point where I thought the glass was going to shatter. (Perhaps that is why there is no demand for these delicacies.)

Finally Jim managed to isolate a sliver of diabetic chocolate and offered it triumphantly to his young neighbour. I suppose it was the years of his parents' careful training that made him reply – most politely – "No, thank you." With a smile Jim popped the chocolate into his own mouth and continued with the rest of the programme.

For those of you who like an end to their stories, let me reassure you that little Peter did take the rest of the Easter egg home with him and that he did eat some of it and he did enjoy it.

The cause of the Miller family's Fix-It going a bit awry must come under the heading "Act of God". It was to have been one of the most carefully prepared surprises we had ever set up, but we failed to invite the Good Lord to our planning meeting.

The whole thing started with one of those attractive letters which, you can tell, come from a lively and loving family. The request came from the daughters of Merchant Navy Officer Jim Miller who, when he was not at sea, lived in Ulverston in Cumbria. With three daughters aged nine, eleven and fifteen their dad used to complain that there was never any peace at mealtimes. There were phone-calls, curlers to put in or take out and a continuous stream of visiting friends. I think he longed for the calm of his floating dining-room somewhere in mid-ocean. His regular complaint was: "It would be more peaceful to have lunch in the middle of Euston station!" The girls decided to put his protestation to the test and asked if Jim could fix it for their father to have a meal in the middle of Euston station so that he could make the comparison.

We were not going to let Jim Miller have this meal all by himself; we wanted all the family involved. The plan was somehow to get him on the 8.08 a.m. from Oxenholme to Euston. As soon as he had left home, Jeanette, our researcher, would appear in a fast car and whisk the three girls and their mother to Manchester airport for them to fly to Heathrow in London, from where they would take a taxi to Euston station. British Rail catering would be ready to serve an excellent three-course meal near the exit from platform seven as soon as Jim's train came in. Having left his family at home he would come directly to London by fast train and see his family already there, waiting for him to join them for lunch in the middle of the busy concourse.

David Whillier, aged eleven, spent a day as butler to the Marquis of Hertford in the magnificent Ragley Hall.

We would not have been able to set this up but for the great co-operation which Jim's employers, Maersk, gave us. They invented a conference which Jim was requested to attend. To make sure he went by train, they sent him a rail warrant and told him, "You will be met at Euston station."

The only thing that was wrong with our planning was the date on which we decided to play the trick. It was Friday, October 16th, 1987, which anyone who lives south of Birmingham should remember as the day of the hurricanes. Early on the morning of that day Jim Miller left home as planned and went to the station in fine weather. Surprisingly the rest of the family got to Heathrow airport and from there to Euston station, although their flight was a bit bumpy towards the end. Dad's train, however, only got as far south as Preston, Lancashire. The storms had flattened miles of the railway's overhead electric cables. He returned home to an empty house and decided his family had been kidnapped.

For me in Twickenham, Middlesex, there were no local trains and no question of using the car. Our road was full of fallen trees, several of them on neighbours' cars. I walked seven miles to Shepherd's Bush, from where I managed to get the underground to Euston. The film crew had made it by car. The station was almost deserted, but in the middle of the concourse was a beautifully laid dining table and the gallant British Rail catering staff were standing by.

It seemed the best plan was to film the meal anyway. The girls drank a toast to their father and Kirstin, the eldest, looked at the camera, as she said, "Sorry you couldn't make it, Dad, but at least you'll have had a meal in peace today!"

Q: WHICH FIX-ITS HAVE BEEN THE MOST POPULAR?

It amazes and delights me when people remember items from old *Jim'll Fix It* programmes, especially when they talk about events which took place years ago. Those which stick in people's minds most are not usually the spectacular or extravagant items we strive for, but odd moments of joy or laughter which have occurred within our Fix-Its. It seems to me that the two most referred to items both happened over ten years ago. One was the case of Lucy Thompson from Andover. We had fixed it for her to be tracked by a bloodhound and, having first checked with her parents that they had the space and means to cope with it, presented Lucy with a bloodhound puppy as a surprise in the studio. It was the look of disbelief on Lucy's face, followed by her tears of happiness, which left such a vivid picture in viewers' minds.

Another oft-mentioned Fix-It was the case of the Second Sutton Cub Scout group. They had written asking Jim to find them somewhere unusual to have their lunch. It was part of an initiative competition. Blackpool Pleasure Beach had been in touch with us, offering their new attraction, "The Revolution", which

One of our best-remembered Fix-Its: Lucy Thompson with bloodhound and handler.

was then the only fairground ride in the country in which the unfortunate passengers travelled upside down. I suggested that the Cubs might like to try and eat their lunch upside down aboard the Revolution and their Akela bravely accepted the offer. Again it was the giggling happy faces of the participants which have stuck in some memories. Perhaps next year we should try to present somebody with a puppy while they are travelling upside down on a rollercoaster.

Q: HAS DOING A FIX-IT EVER GOT YOU INTO TROUBLE?

Yes. One episode particularly sticks in my mind. A brave lady from Hastings named Jane had expressed an unusual desire. She wanted to walk along to the end of the jib on one of those giant building site cranes. We approached a large construction company, who offered us the use of one of their sites, which was to be a new courthouse in Maidstone. The way things finished up on this Fix-It, they could have been getting that courthouse ready for me.

We had taken every safety precaution. Our Fixee was at all times accompanied by the foreman and was always attached to the crane by a safety-harness. She and the foreman took the elevator up to the cab, where she chatted with the friendly driver. Then she and the foreman edged their way towards the tip of the jib arm. I hardly need say that our volunteer had a good head for heights, but even she had to admit it was quite a dizzying experience. The crane's upright tower sways to and fro from the vertical and the jib sways up and down from the horizontal. The result for anyone standing on the arm is a constant yaw and the further you go along the arm, the greater it becomes. When they reached the end of the jib Jane's courage was tested even further. "Would you like to go for a little ride now?" was the offer. Jane accepted and thrilled to a three-hundred-and-sixty-degree aerial tour of Maidstone and its environs.

That would have been the end of the story had not the friendly crane-driver stuck some snapshots commemorating the event on the wall of his cab. Some weeks later came the day for the visit to the site of the Factories Inspectorate. They are the people who check that employers are adhering to the Factories Act, which was designed to protect the health and safety of employees. An in-

The forbidden ride: Jane's crane.

Buck's Fizz plus one.

spector saw the snapshots and enquired about them. The cheerful crane-driver told the inspector the tale of their *Jim'll Fix It* day, including the bit about the joyride ... If this bit had been a movie drama, there would now have been a heavy minor chord from a piano, accompanied by a close-up of the inspector, narrowing his eyes. We had transgressed the Factories Act, clause fourteen, section eleven, subsection two, brackets, conveyance of persons on moving cranes, derricks and gantries, end brackets.

The man from the construction company telephoned me urgently. "You and I could go to jail for this, you know," he said.

"But we can't undo the ride," I replied in some alarm. "We have caused her to commit the offence. What do we do?"

It transpired that the solution was to have lunch with the Inspectorate. The BBC laid on its grade A hospitality for a viewing of the offending film. It seems there are a fair number of factory inspectors and quite a lot of them turned up for the free lunch.

First there was a viewing and then a conference. A curious compromise was reached whereby the whole episode would be forgotten if the film of the rotating crane was never transmitted. It seemed to me rather like saying to a convicted murderer, "We'll let you go free, provided that you never let anyone know that you did it."

Anyway it got me off the hook, unless writing this story has put me back on the hook. I made a point of not joining the inspectors for the lunch, saying that I had now to go and find another story to replace the one they had removed. I do not think any of the inspectors noticed.

Q: WHAT IS THE FUNNIEST REQUEST YOU HAVE RECEIVED?

Probably this one:

Dear Jim,

Please would you fix it for my mum to go into one of your hospitals to get me a wee baby brother. I have three big sisters, so I want to be a big sister as well.

I know you can fix anything, so please fix this for my mum.

I haven't told her about this letter yet, as I want her to get a big surprise.

Love from Gillian

But I have a soft spot for this one:

Dear Jim,

My colleagues at work say I couldn't organise a piss-up in a brewery. Please fix it for me to prove them wrong.

It was decided not to pursue the idea.

"If you go down to the woods today, you're sure of a big surprise."

The Jordan family complained to Jim that ghost trains were not scary enough. We gave them one with living "ghosts".

The locomotive and the St Trinians Fixees are in fact travelling away from the camera for safety reasons. For transmission, the film will be shown backwards.

Sample Survey

Out of one thousand randomly selected letters the biggest single subject category was sport with 178 requests. Ninety-eight of these concerned football and a surprising twenty-three related to the *World Wrestling Federation* as seen exclusively on Sky satellite television.

This is the breakdown of the eighty-seven letters about transport in one form or another:

Aircraft (including 12 hot air balloons, 11 Concordes and 3 helicopters) 51

Cars 19

Trains 11

Motorbikes 4

Lorries 2

Requests about animals accounted for exactly one hundred letters. Thirty-five were about horses (all but one from females) and twelve for swimming with dolphins. Fishing, which is supposedly the most popular hobby, was the subject of nine letters, the same number as people wanting to join the police. Twenty-one wanted to get involved in modelling, ten in hairdressing. Fourteen wanted to do something with the forces, the same number as wanted to play doctors and nurses. Forty correspondents wrote about the movies, nine of them with the perennial desire to indulge in some "Dirty Dancing" with Patrick Swayze. Twenty were to do with the preparation or serving of food. There were only five ballet dancers in this batch and three young hopefuls wanting to be bridesmaids. The smallest group I could call a category were the two letters about gardening.

Complaint

"Why won't Jim fix it for me?" complains ninety-two-year-old the Reverend Ted Royds-Jones. He has in fact already earned a *Jim'll Fix It* badge, when back in 1983 he looped the loop as a passenger in a glider when he was a mere eighty-four. He now wants to do a parachute jump, but is aware that the Fix-It team seems to be dragging its feet on the matter. "Surely it would be all right if I jumped into the sea," says Ted. He is such a delightful man and a wonderful sport, that I am trying to persuade him to come up with another idea for a Fix-It – something a little less energetic.

DO YOU WANT A GO?

All the right ingredients: tea-time with Hercules the Bear.

If reading this book has made you decide you might like to have something fixed for you, may I offer some tips aimed at increasing your chances of success.

Remember that, although the programme is about dreams coming true, its real objective is to entertain its viewers. The requests we satisfy need to make interesting television. Having a meal in the best restaurant in the world is likely to be a very pleasant experience. Watching someone else eat it is likely to be less rewarding. So, unless you have only one obsessive dream in your head, make your Fix-It request something that might be fun for other people to watch, such as telling a taxi-driver "Follow that cab!", riding a camel race or taking part in a Zulu war dance. Those are all things we have done. So do not ask for them. We try not to repeat ourselves. We get quite a few letters which say, "Please fix it for me to do so-and-so like the girl did on *Jim'll Fix It* last night."

I believe ideally a Fix-It fulfilment should give rise to these four comments from viewers:

> Isn't she having fun?
> Isn't she brave?
> Isn't she lucky?
> Isn't it funny?

I do not know if we have ever satisfied all those criteria in one Fix-It. Perhaps having a private tea party with Hercules the Bear got near to the mark.

Generally speaking a letter is more likely to be successful if it is for one person. I believe on the whole audiences prefer to concentrate on a single person's experience rather than that of two or more. It is also a consideration that it is more complicated and expensive to organise two or more Fixees and their families than one. There have been several occasions on which we have had to reject a request we would otherwise have fixed, simply because it was for two or more people.

Write your address on the letter. It is surprising how many people do not. I guess they sometimes write their addresses on the back of the envelope, but that is no good to us, since the letters have been separated from their envelopes before we read them.

The more popular the thing you ask for is, the greater the number of people there will be asking for it. That is going to reduce the chances of your letter being picked. Try for the number three rock band instead of the number one.

A request for a pleasant surprise for a friend or relation stands a better chance than most things. Good funny ideas are the tops. For example, some applicants have asked to put well-known sayings to the test. The father of young Kelvin had said – rather unkindly – that he did not think his son could fight his way out of a paper bag. Kelvin wanted the chance to prove that his dad was wrong and asked Jim to come to the rescue. The programme set up a full-size boxing ring in the studio and provided Kelvin with a referee, a second and, of course, a giant paper bag. A bag that is six foot by four foot has to be made of fairly tough paper and on the night Kelvin's brown paper opponent put up a pretty good struggle.

But, after about two minutes a small rip appeared in the side of the writhing bundle and finally Kelvin emerged triumphant. The remains of the paper bag lay sadly crumpled on the canvas as the referee counted it out and Kelvin was declared the winner. His letter was such an original idea it stood out like a diamond in a coalmine.

Is Kelvin the only person to have fought his way out of a paper bag, I wonder, and how many people have actually found a needle in a haystack? That is what Katie and Nicola wanted to do and discovered from the Yorkshire Museum of Farming that the saying has more meaning than most of us realise. Historically plenty of people have lost – and presumably found – needles in haystacks. A hay "needle" is like a six-foot-long poker with a hook on the end. A farmer would stick it into the side of a stack and the hook would secure for him a sample from deep inside the pile of hay. In that way the farmer would know if the hay from inside the stack was of the same quality as that on the outside.

Once you let go of its handle, even a six-foot needle is nigh on impossible to find inside a few tons of hay, as Katie and Nicola soon discovered. The museum staff had built an old-style rick for them and the girls had to cover their eyes and count to ten while the needle was hidden. The staff let the girls search for half an hour without success and then introduced a bit of modern technology, a metal detector. Once they had mastered the electronic device, it took only minutes for the girls to fulfil their desire and find a needle in a haystack.

Another eye-catching request came from Keith Attwood of Burton-on-Trent, requiring heavy security. His loving parents had told him that he was worth his weight in gold and Keith wanted to know what that weight in gold

93

Nanette Newman wonders how many plates this bubble would wash.

would be worth in money. The Bank of England kindly offered to lend us the gold on the not surprising condition that we went to them rather than they brought it to us. The biggest problem was finding a pair of scales of sufficient size to take a boy on one side and a pile of gold on the other. A modern digital weighing machine, albeit very accurate, would not have the same dramatic effect as a good, old-fashioned balance. The researcher managed to track down the very thing, courtesy of the Museum of London: an old pair of scales, once used for the weighing of spices and rescued from a docklands warehouse before its conversion to modern dwellings.

Keith sat down on the left-hand tray and some very large security men watched with eagle eyes as first one and then two twenty-eight-pound gold bars were placed on the other side of the scales. Keith was still the heavier and a third gold bar was added.

Now the gold was heavier. The third bar was taken off again and gold sovereigns (worth sixty-three pounds each) were added until the scales finally balanced. Keith's weight was equal to two gold bars and five hundred and forty-one sovereigns. If, as he had been told, he was worth his weight in gold, Keith's value was two hundred and fifty-four thousand, eight hundred and one pounds and fourteen pence, "at today's prices", as the man from the Bank added.

I hope that some of you having read that will now come up with some original ideas which will keep us fixing it for years to come.